To Anna Peirce

CONTENTS

1 *In the beginning*
(and then later on) 6

2 *On the road- points south* 12

3 *The "un"common house lobster* 26

4 *In the field*
(and other places)
lobsters in their environment 44

5 *Strange but true* 56

6 *Getting closer* 74

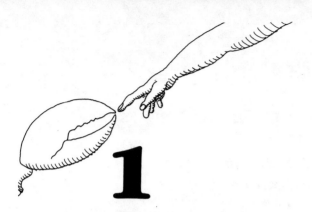

1

In the beginning
(and then later on)

Lobster ancestors were covered with fur, walked on their back legs, slightly stooped over, and carried little clubs.

LOBSTER TALES

by

David Hurley

Down East Books
Camden, Maine

Copyright © 1997 by David Hurley
All rights reserved.

Originally published in 1991 by *Yankee* Books

Printed by Versa Press, Inc. East Peoria, Illinois
4   3   2   1

Down East Books
Camden, Maine
Book Orders: 800-685-7962
www.downeastbooks.com
a division of Down East Enterprise,
publishers of *Down East* magazine

ISBN: 0-89272-670-9

Library of Congress Control Number: 2004106344

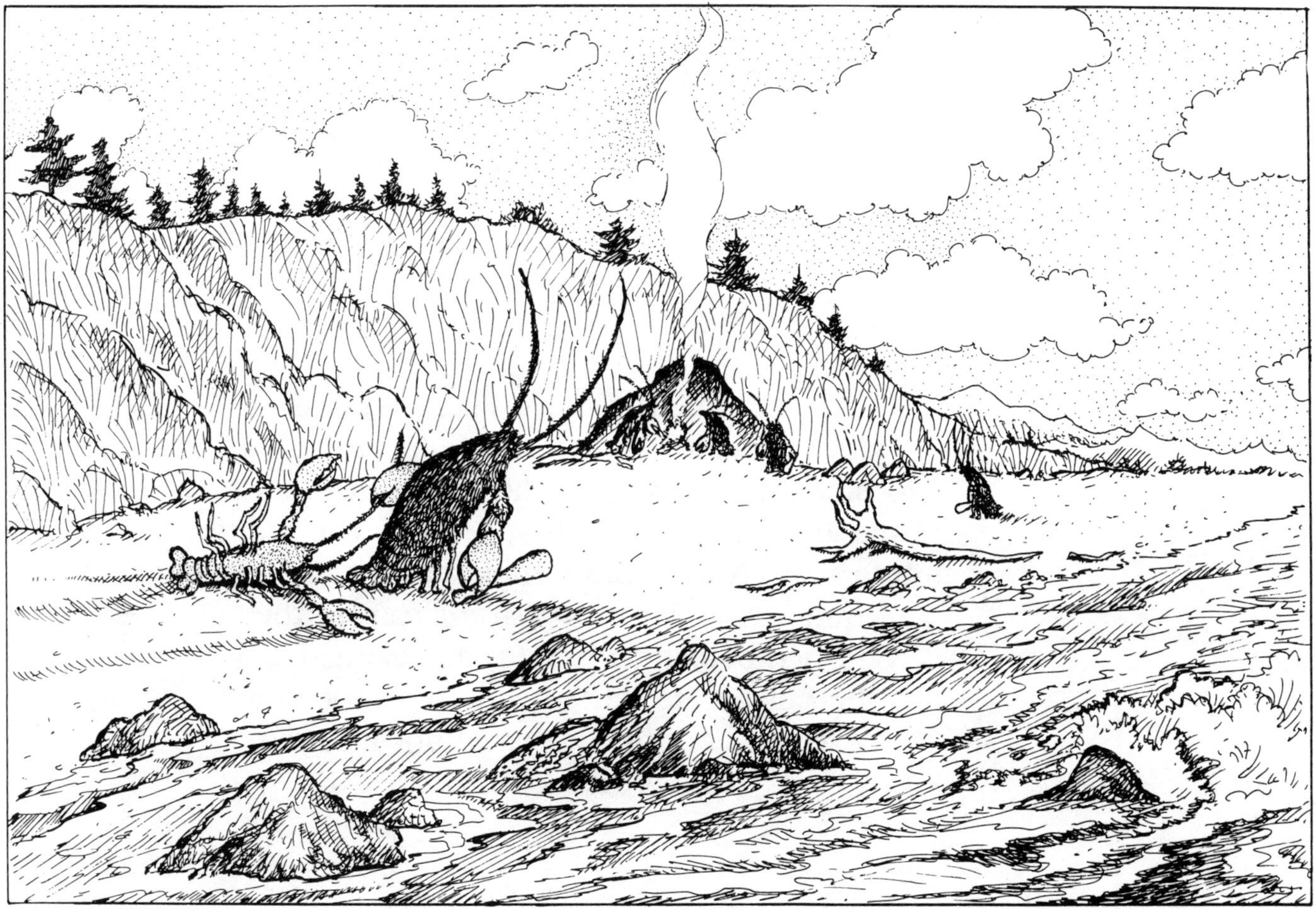

At one time the Great Plains were dotted with prairie lobster colonies. Presumably the lobsters had adapted to this environment when the great inland seas disappeared. The prairie lobsters survived because their claws made digging quite easy. For no apparent reason, they vanished before the white man came, leaving their elaborate settlements to prairie dogs, who were quite lazy and not inclined to dig their own homes.

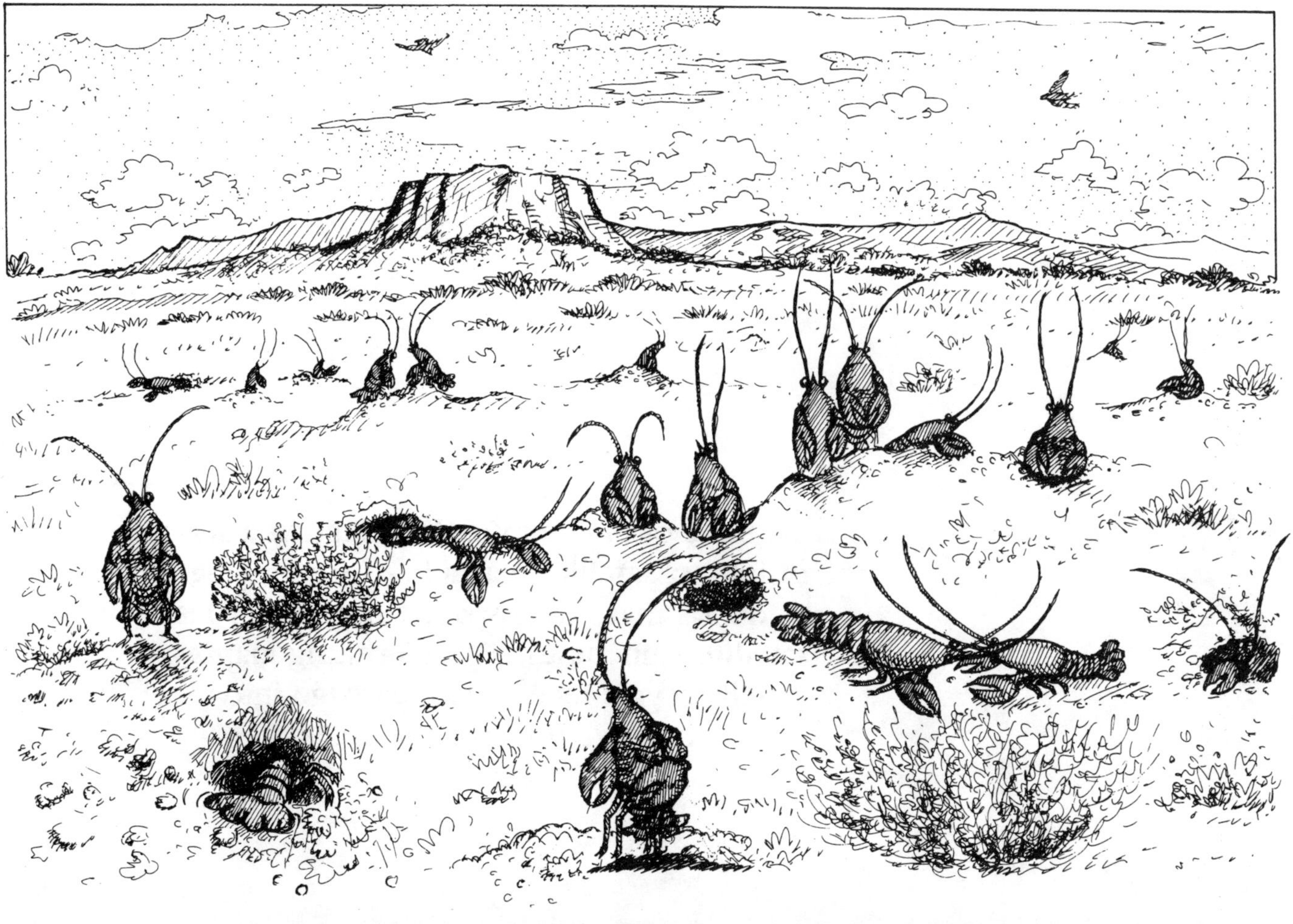

The State of Maine intends to launch a series
of lobster satellites capable of scavenging
the debris that litters space from numerous
satellite launchings. These orbiting giants
will recycle metal space-garbage into
valuable mineral resources.

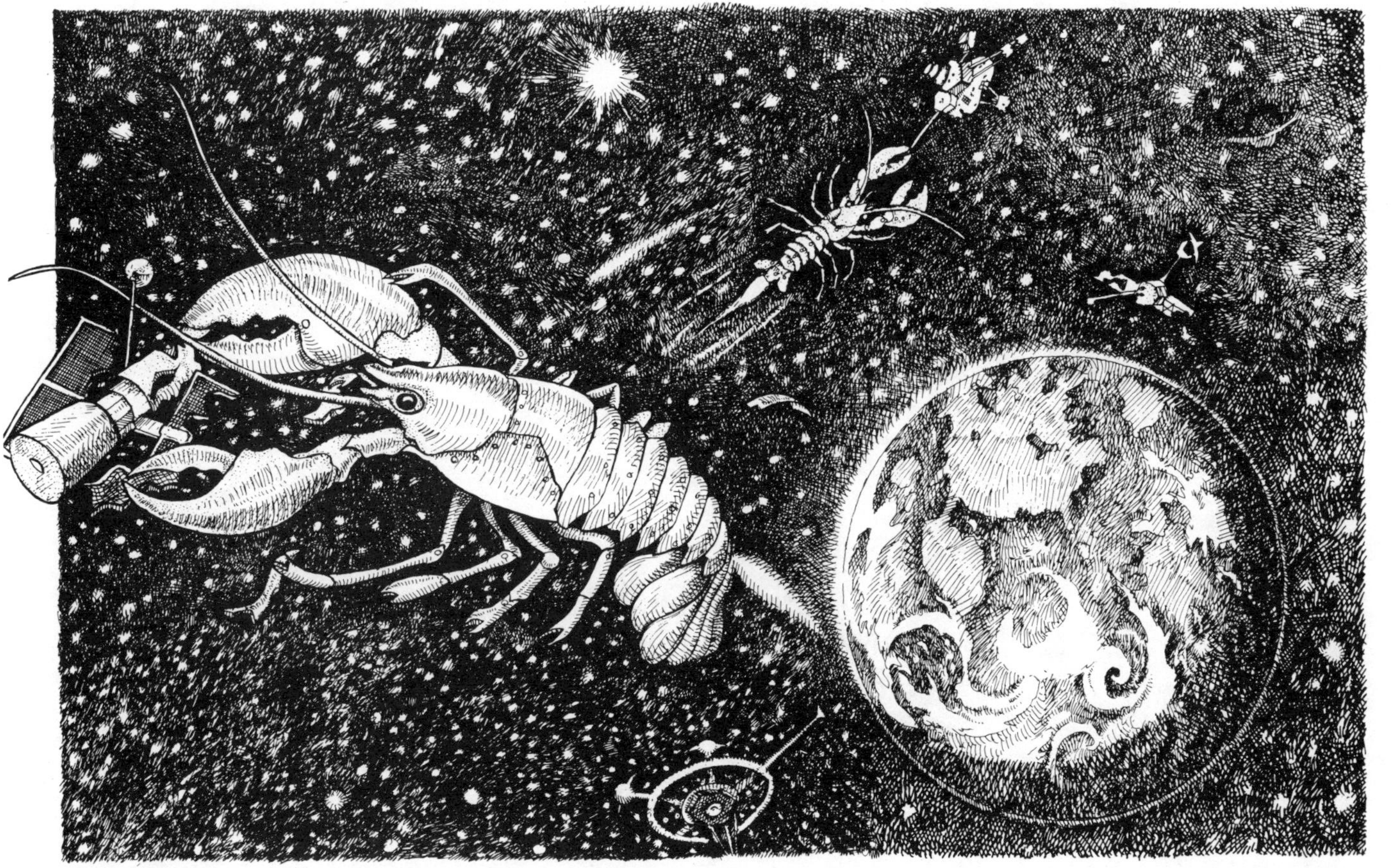

In the future . . .

2

On the road—points south

Each autumn the familiar sight and sound of ducks and geese flying south fill the air. A closer look at some of those "V" formations reveals that this is also the season when lobsters head for points south and warmer temperatures.

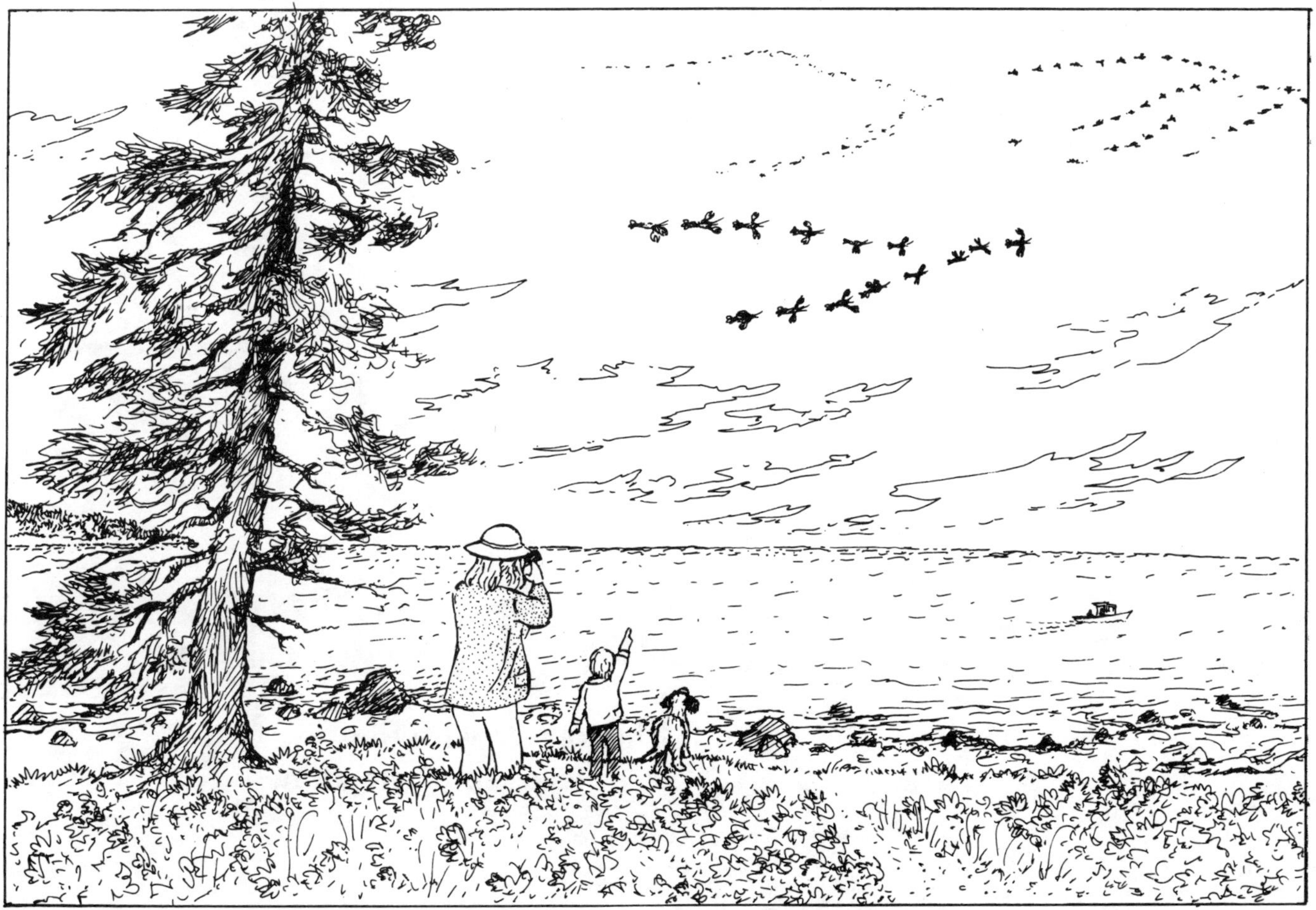

The lobster who flies the fastest
leads the formation.

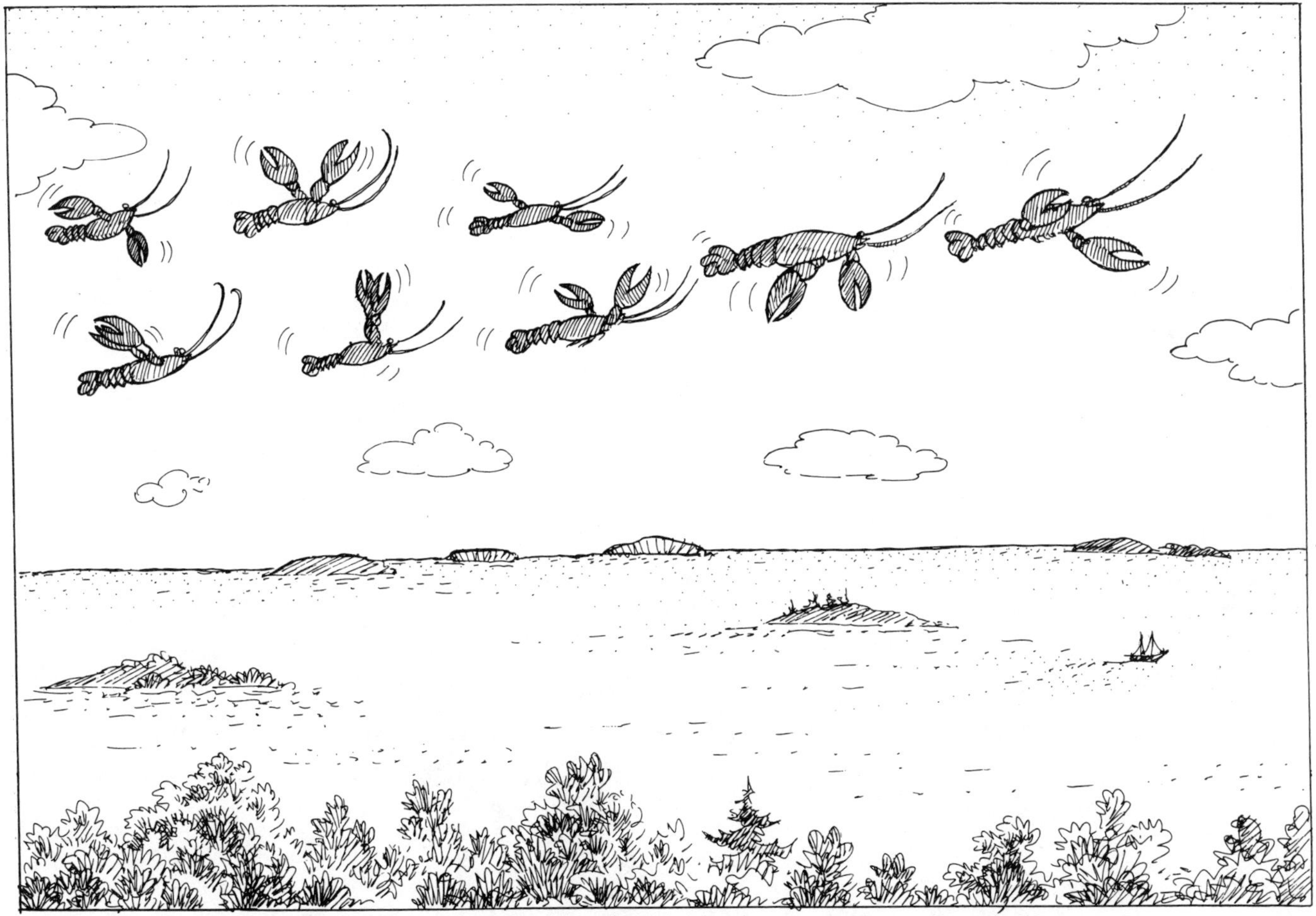

As the lobsters fly south,
they often molt along the way, discarding
their shells in various locations.

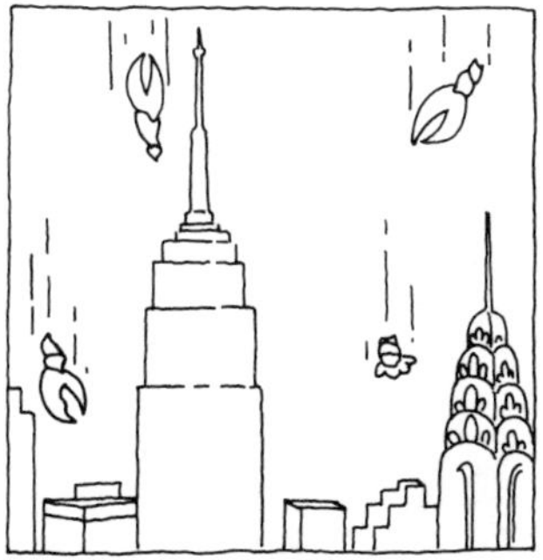

The Empire State Building

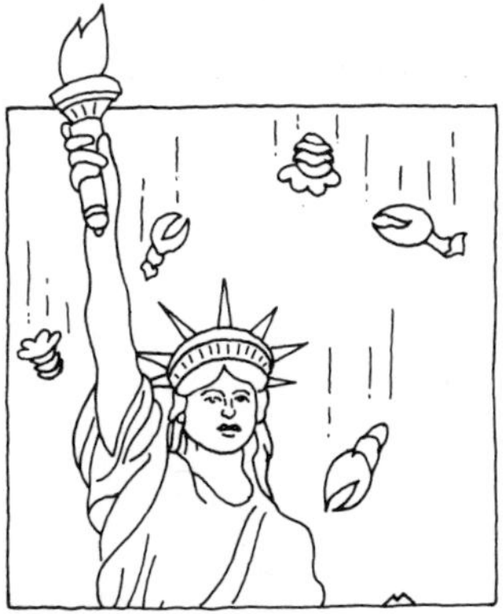

The Statue of Liberty

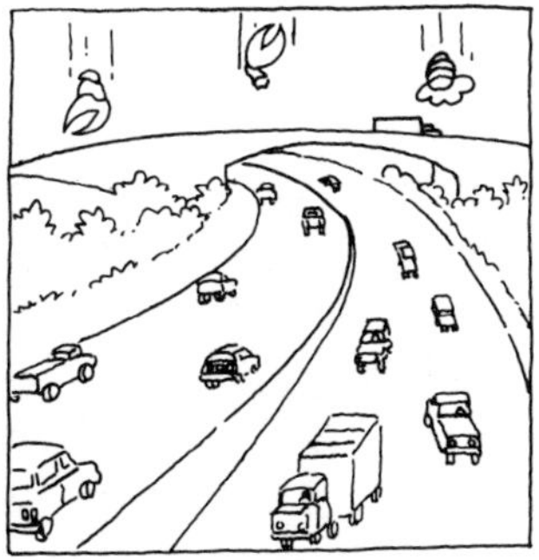

The Long Island Expressway

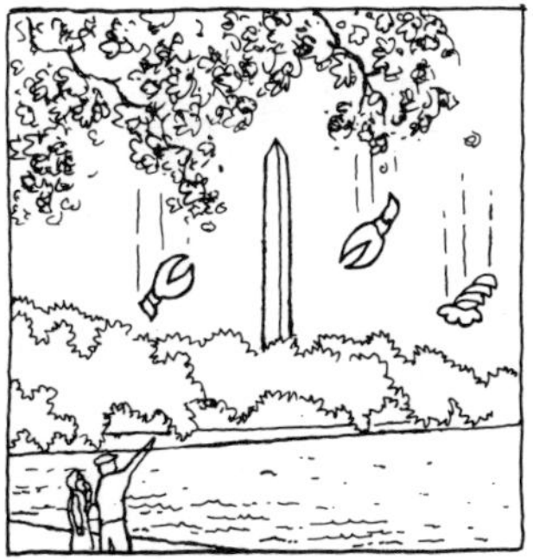

The Washington Monument

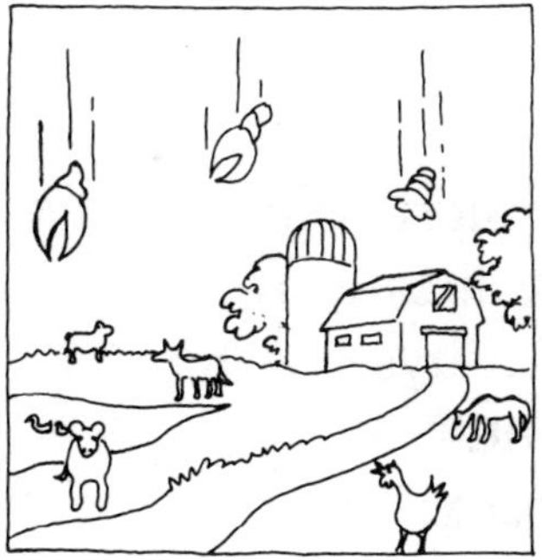

Farmlands

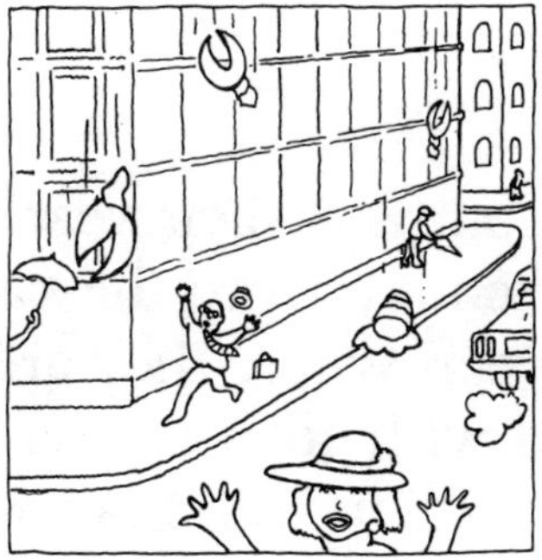

Downtown metropolitan areas

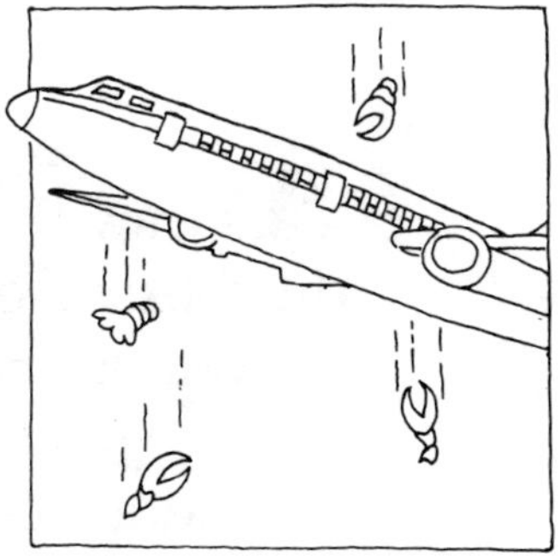

"Ladies and gentlemen, if you look out your window you will see the shells of migrating lobsters."

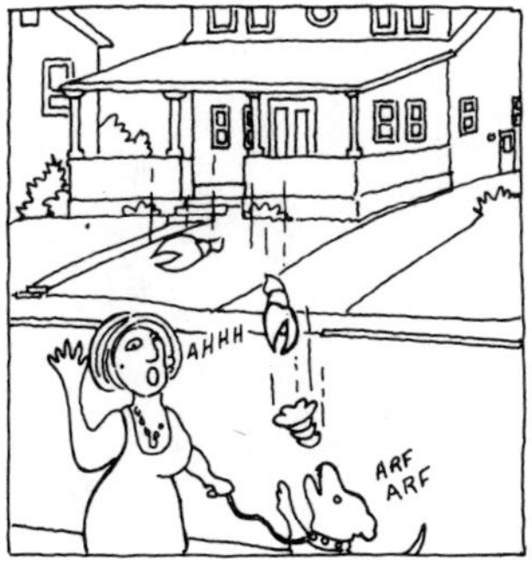
AHHH
ARF ARF

Suburban wastelands

As they fly south on their yearly migration,
the lobsters often return to the same location
year after year, where they are always
greeted with great excitement.
"Mom! Mom! The lobsters are back!"

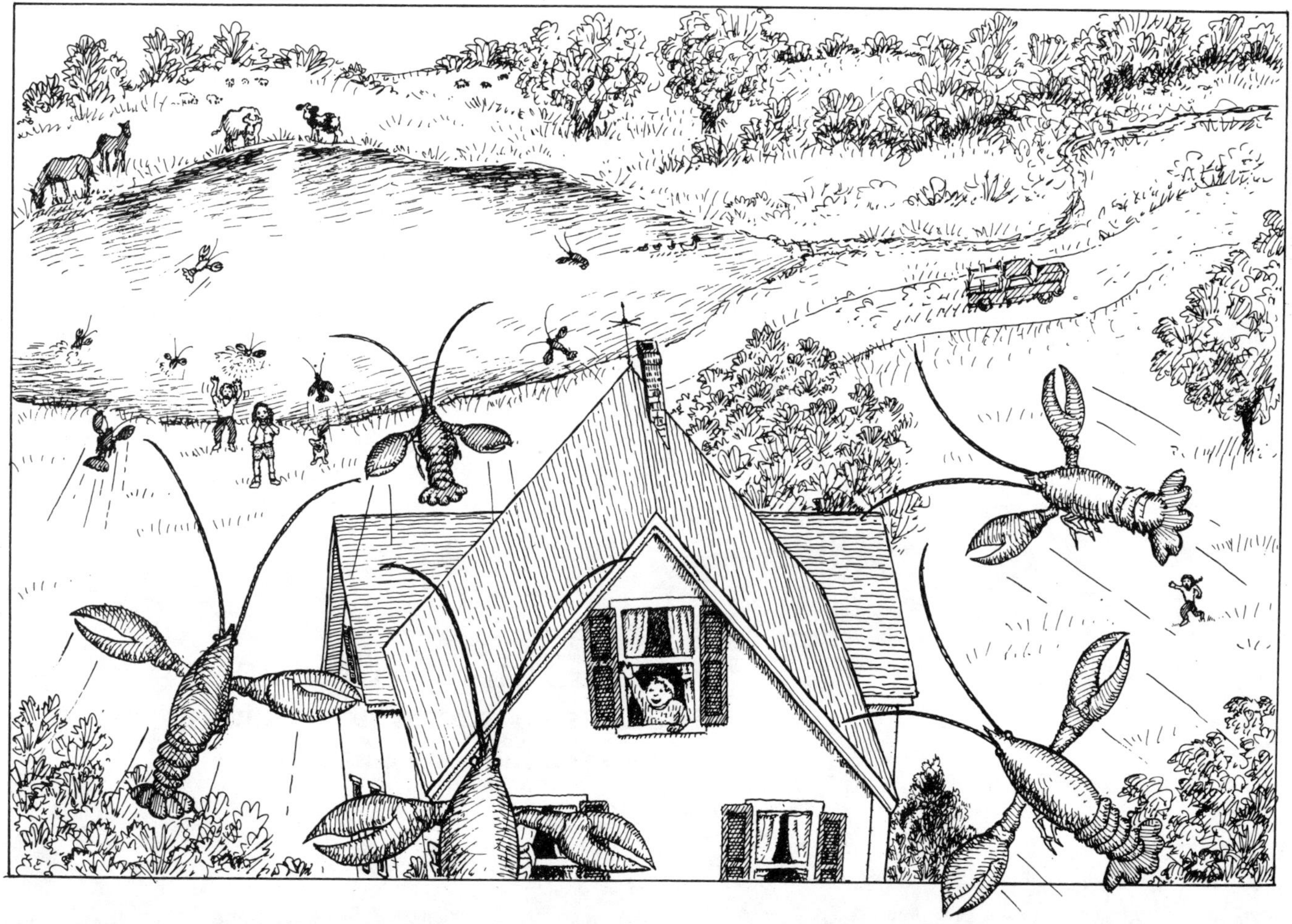

Each year in Florida,
tourists flock to the town squares
to see the returning lobsters.

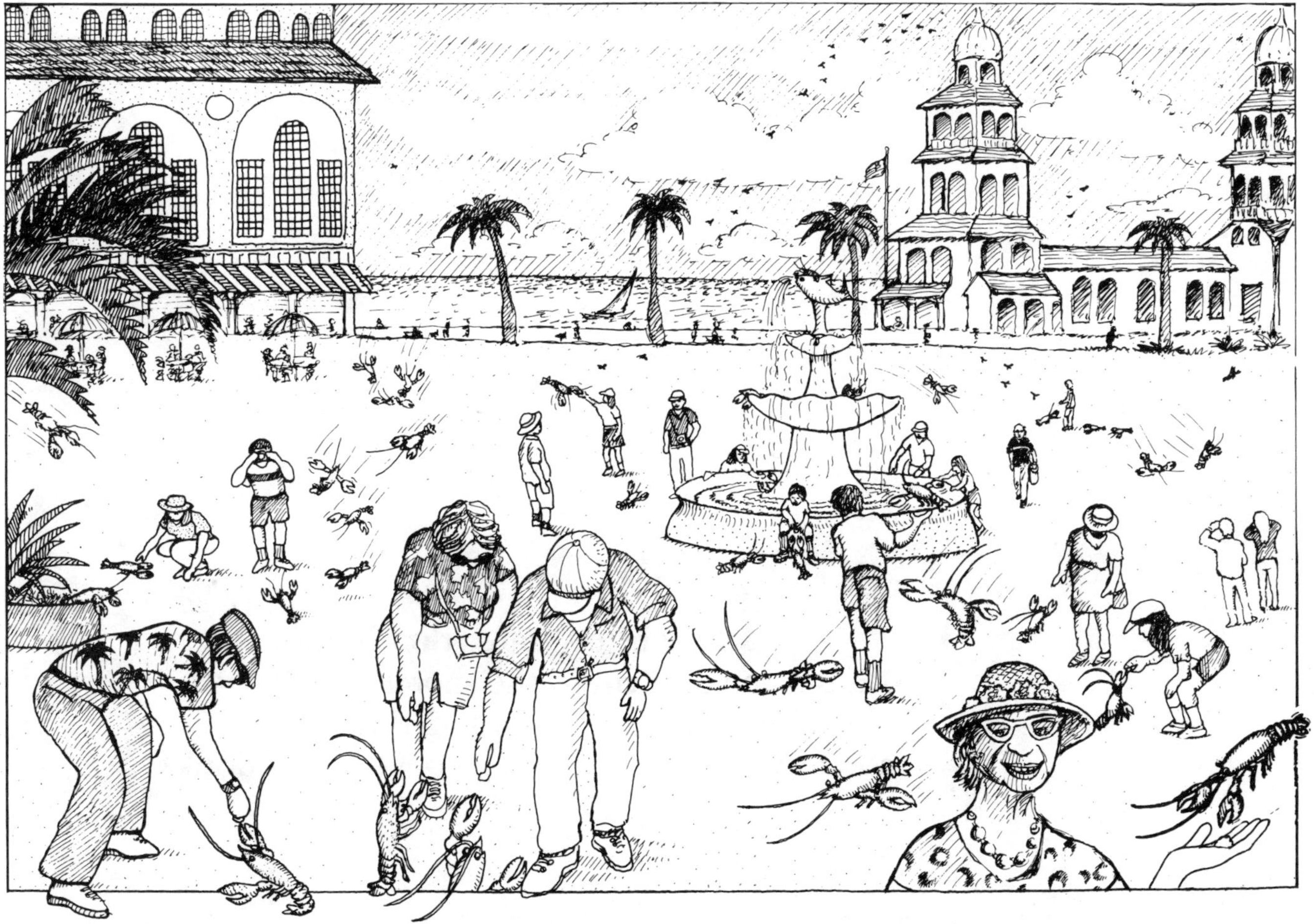

The lobsters' migration south
leads some of them to the shores of Bermuda,
where they enjoy sunning themselves
in lounge chairs and sipping cool tropical drinks.

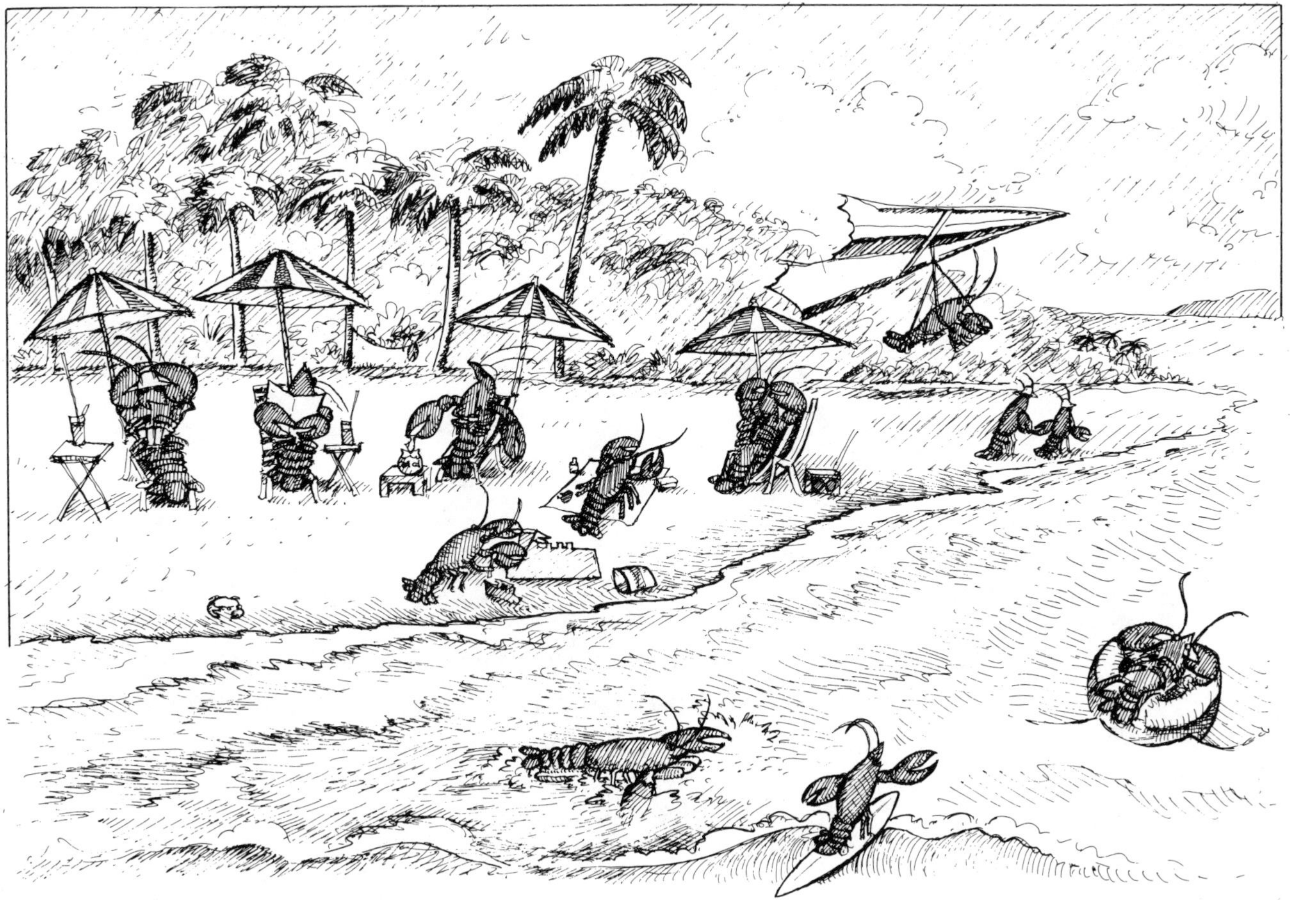

In many cities the price of lobster
is prohibitively high in winter due to the cost
of airfare when they return north
for winter engagements.

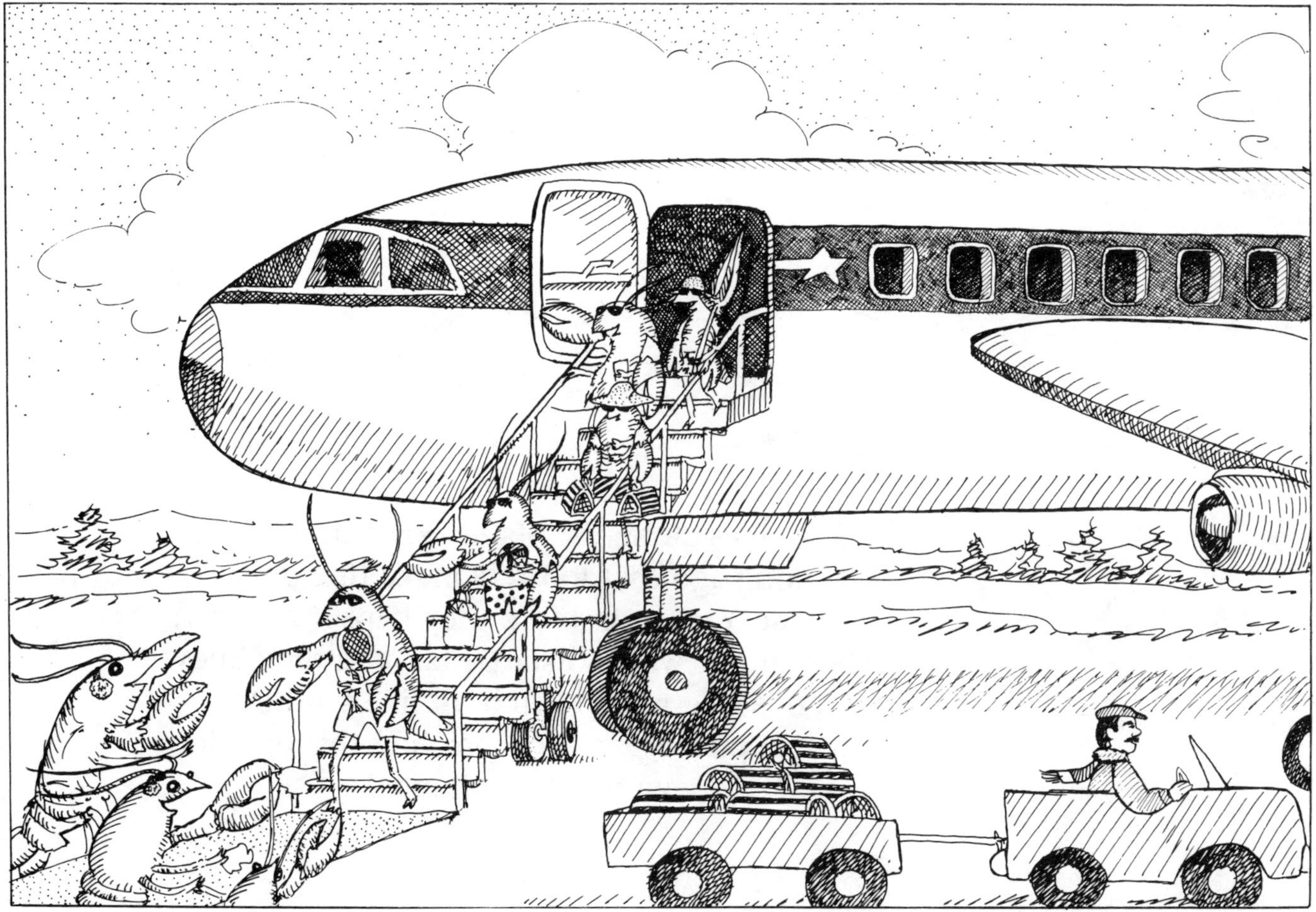

3

The "un"common house lobster

Families along the Maine coast discovered
long ago that lobsters make fine pets.
In true Yankee fashion, they kept it a secret.
They didn't want to start a fad and they knew
this one would catch on like wildfire.
Hence, photographs chronicling this practice
were rarely allowed.

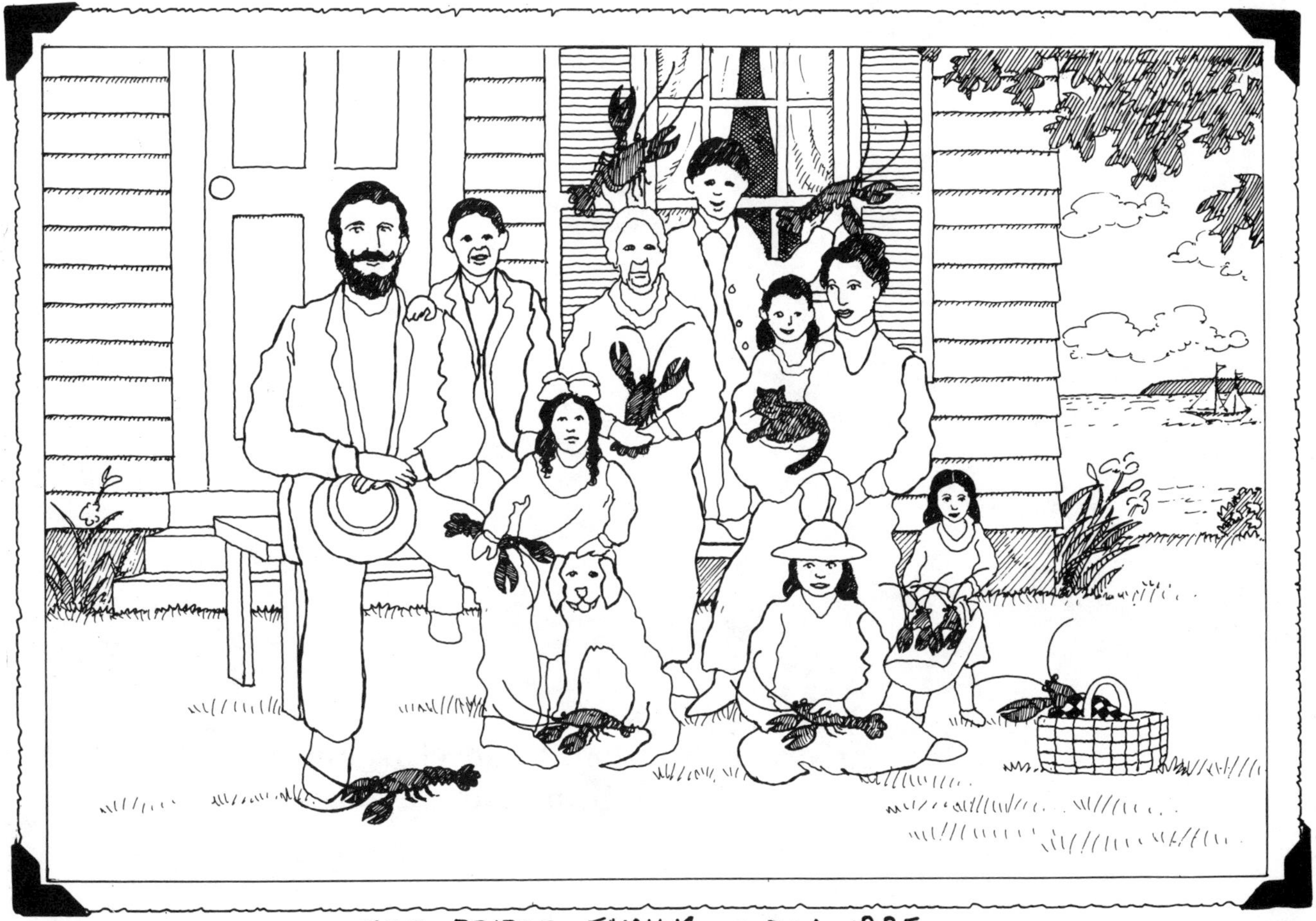

THE PEIRCE FAMILY CIRCA 1885

The lap lobster is a gentle creature that thrives on affection. It especially enjoys being rubbed behind its antennae.

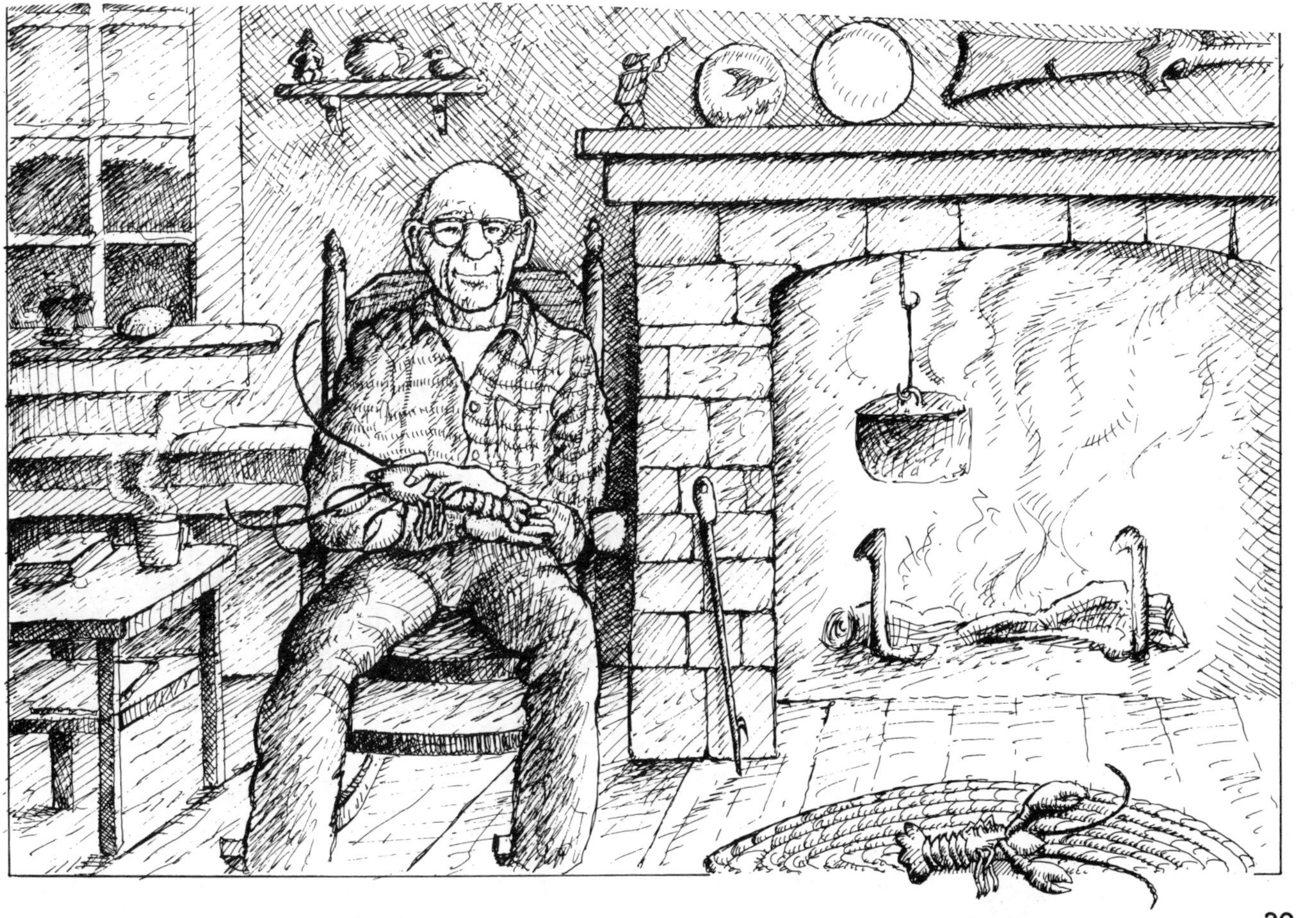

Free Ride

When little lobsters start yelling,"Mom, we're bored, there's nothing to do," then it's time for a trip to the amusement park. Stuffing themselves into the lobster trap, they first eat all the snacks the lobsterman has left for them. Then it's time for a ride to the top. Too small to keep, they. are thrown back into the ocean where they quickly get back in line to do the wild ride over again.

How to cure the lobster "blues."

Place lobster in washing machine.
Add: one cup of salt, some seaweed, assorted food scraps and some "tub" toys.
Put washing machine on cold-water rinse, gentle cycle.

If you have followed directions properly,
you should have a happy lobster in one hour.
Your lobster will be refreshed and revitalized.
This treatment is equivalent to a
one-week trip to Hawaii.
In the future, if your lobster carries
his tub toys to the washing machine and looks
forlorn, you will know what to do.

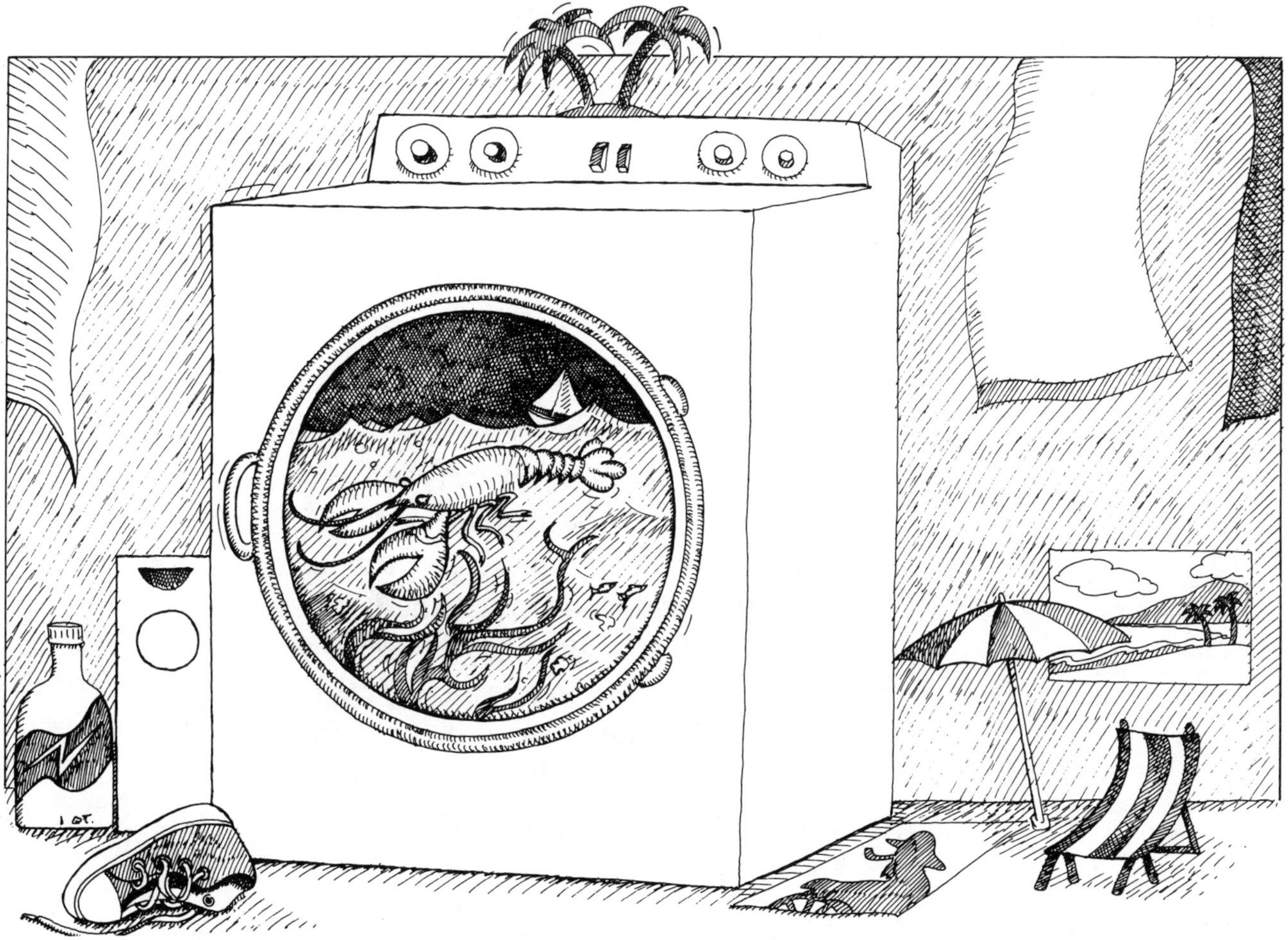
1 QT.

Everyone knows that lobsters are cold-blooded,
but when it comes to displaying affection,
this simply is not true. Eager to please, they often
can be found whining at the back door
awaiting their master's return.
Not only do they respond well to
learning tricks, they also will do odd jobs and
sometimes get a little paper route to help
pay their own way. And unlike other noisy and
messy pets they don't bark or shed hair.

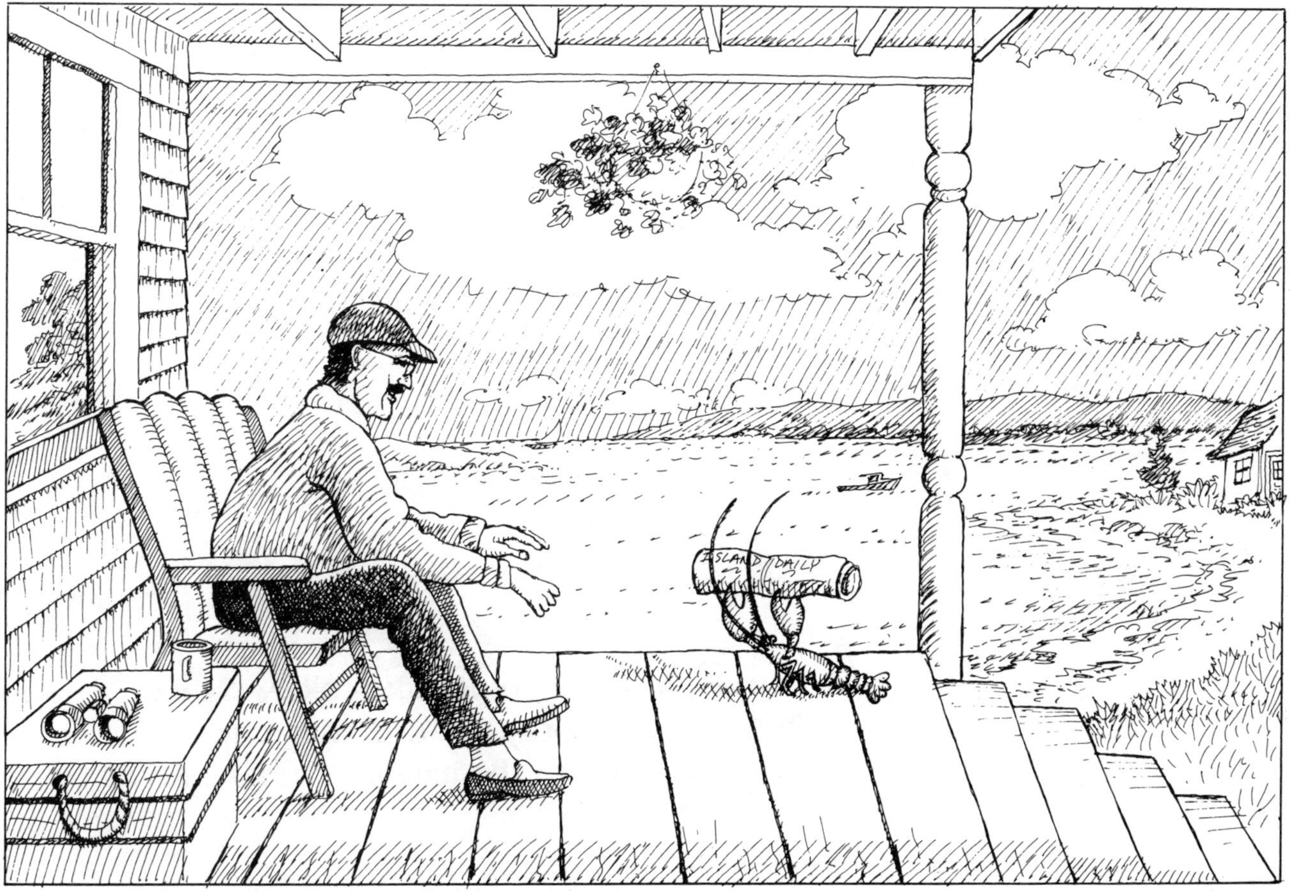
ISLAND DAILY

As a rule, lobsters do not like cold weather.
But, given the proper attire, they can
be coaxed out into the harsher elements.

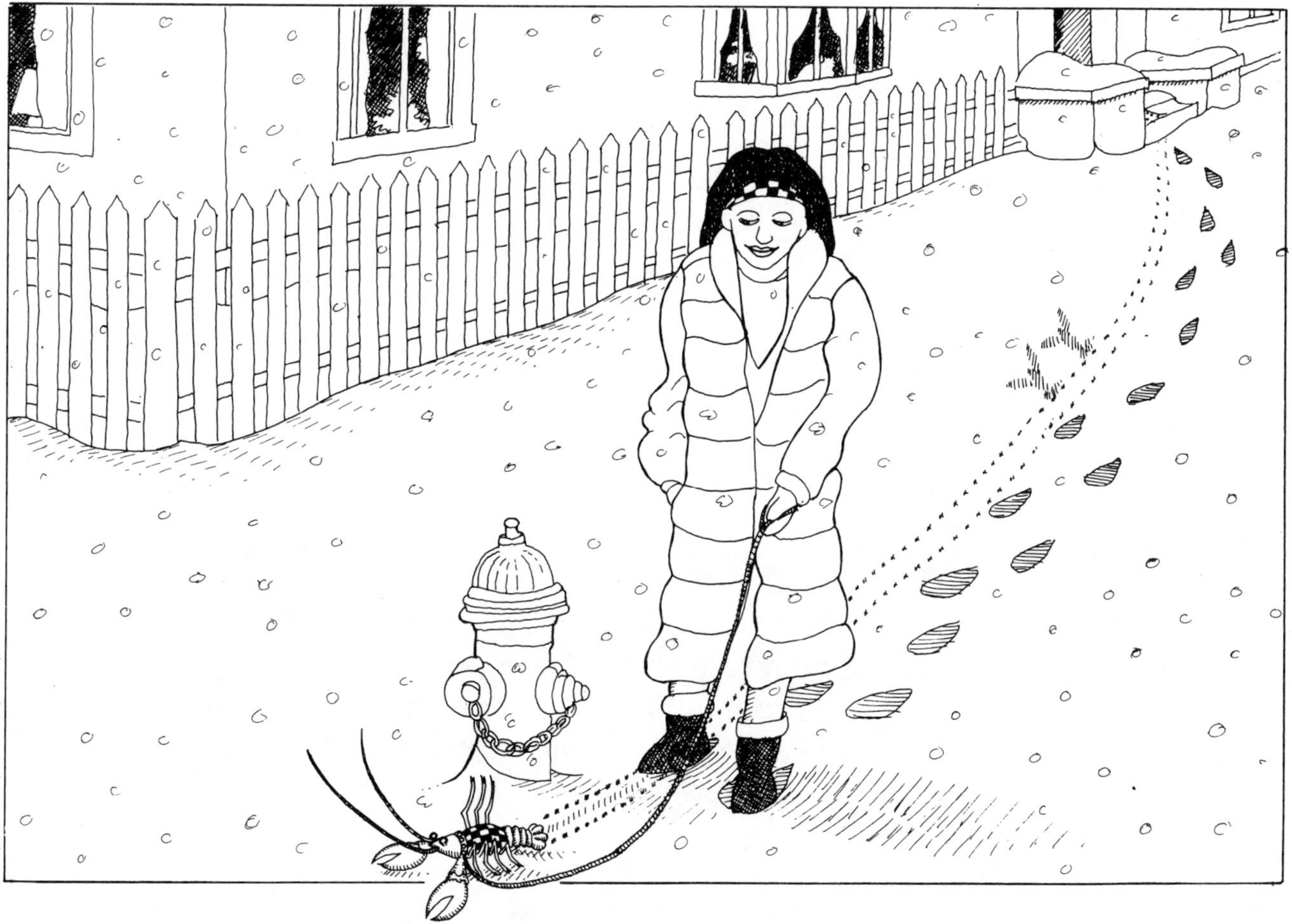

The house lobster's propensity for exploring knows no bounds. They have an uncanny ability to seek out strategic spots where they can leisurely observe house activities.

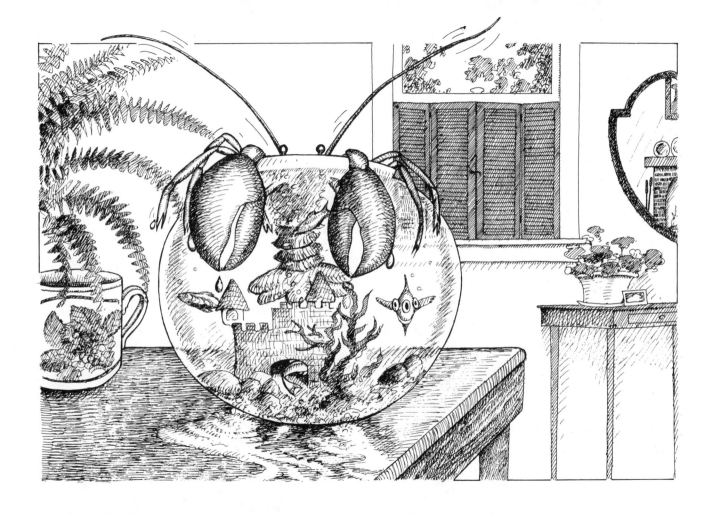

J ust as it is a proven myth that dogs and cats are natural enemies, it is also true that lobsters can be a loving addition to the household.

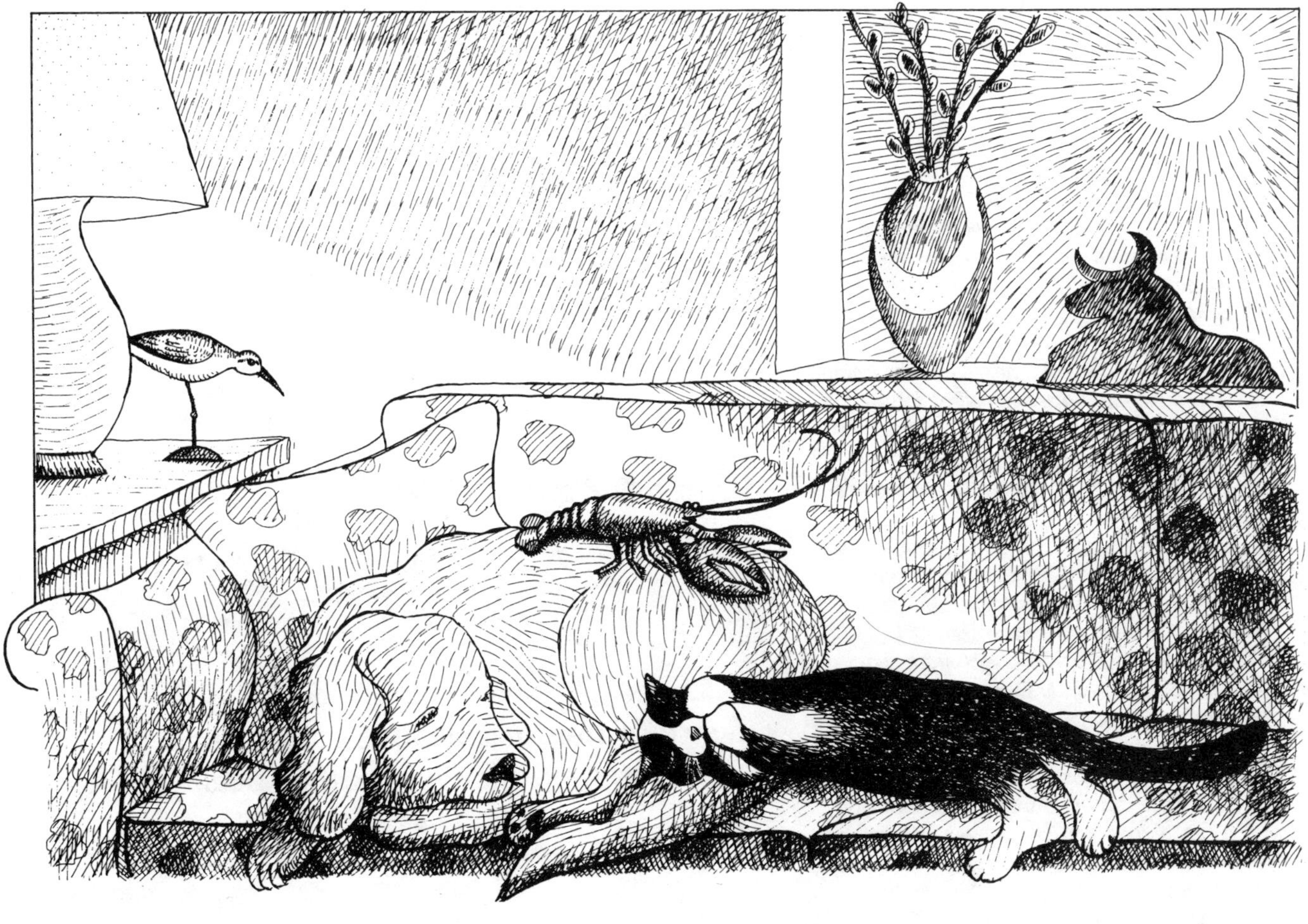

Lobsters have often found their way into the hearts and living rooms of pet owners. People are often pleasantly surprised at how well lobsters can adapt.

Many times a lobster is brought home from the lobster pound destined for a boiling pot of water and literally has only a few moments to turn the cries of, "Let's eat it!" into, "Let's keep it!"

You ask, "How is this done?" Not by whining and whimpering. No self-respecting lobster would resort to begging to have its life spared.

The answer is surprising yet simple. The trick most often used to get a potential pet owner's attention is juggling.

A lobster juggling three or four lemons has a captive audience. This situation provides the opportunity to show other tricks. And thus crucial "pet bonding" begins.

All young lobsters are taught juggling as juveniles. But rarely do they get a chance to display their skills, as the first thing the lobstermen do to a lobster is put rubber bands on their claws, or less recently, barbaric pegs.

"Now we can't very well have a tank of juggling lobsters, can we? Just as well everyone thinks the lobsters are being kept from attacking one another."

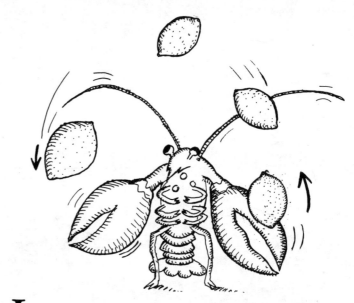

Lobsters have a highly developed sense of humor and love to engage in household play with other pets.

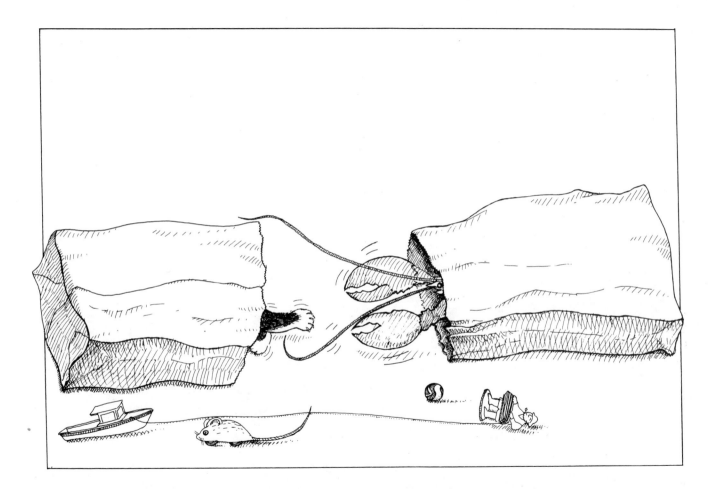

At times there is disagreement
on key issues, such as water rights.

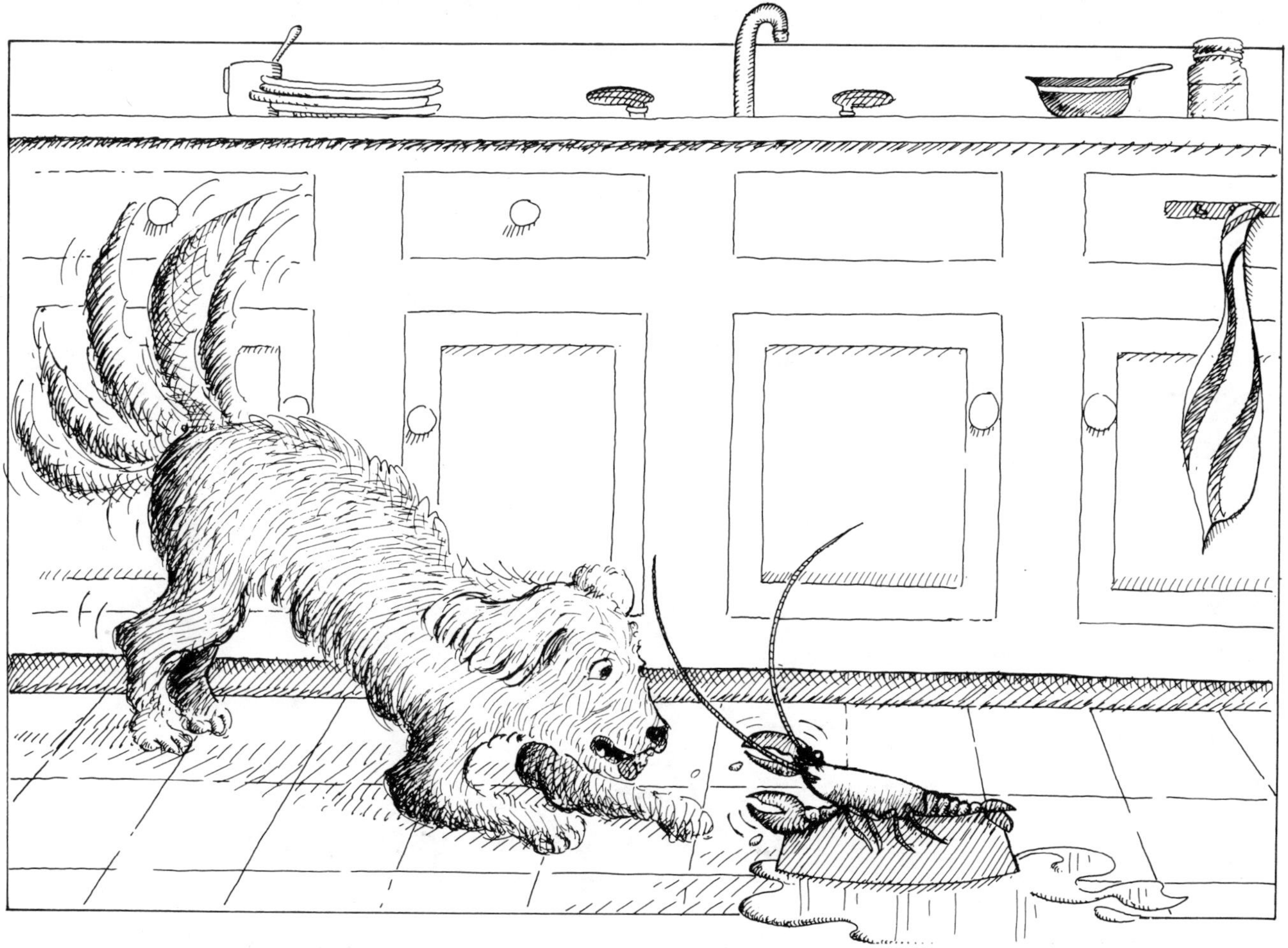

4

In the field
(and other places)—
lobsters in their
environment

Lobsters are very creative creatures.
They enjoy imitating the actions
of other animals in their environment.

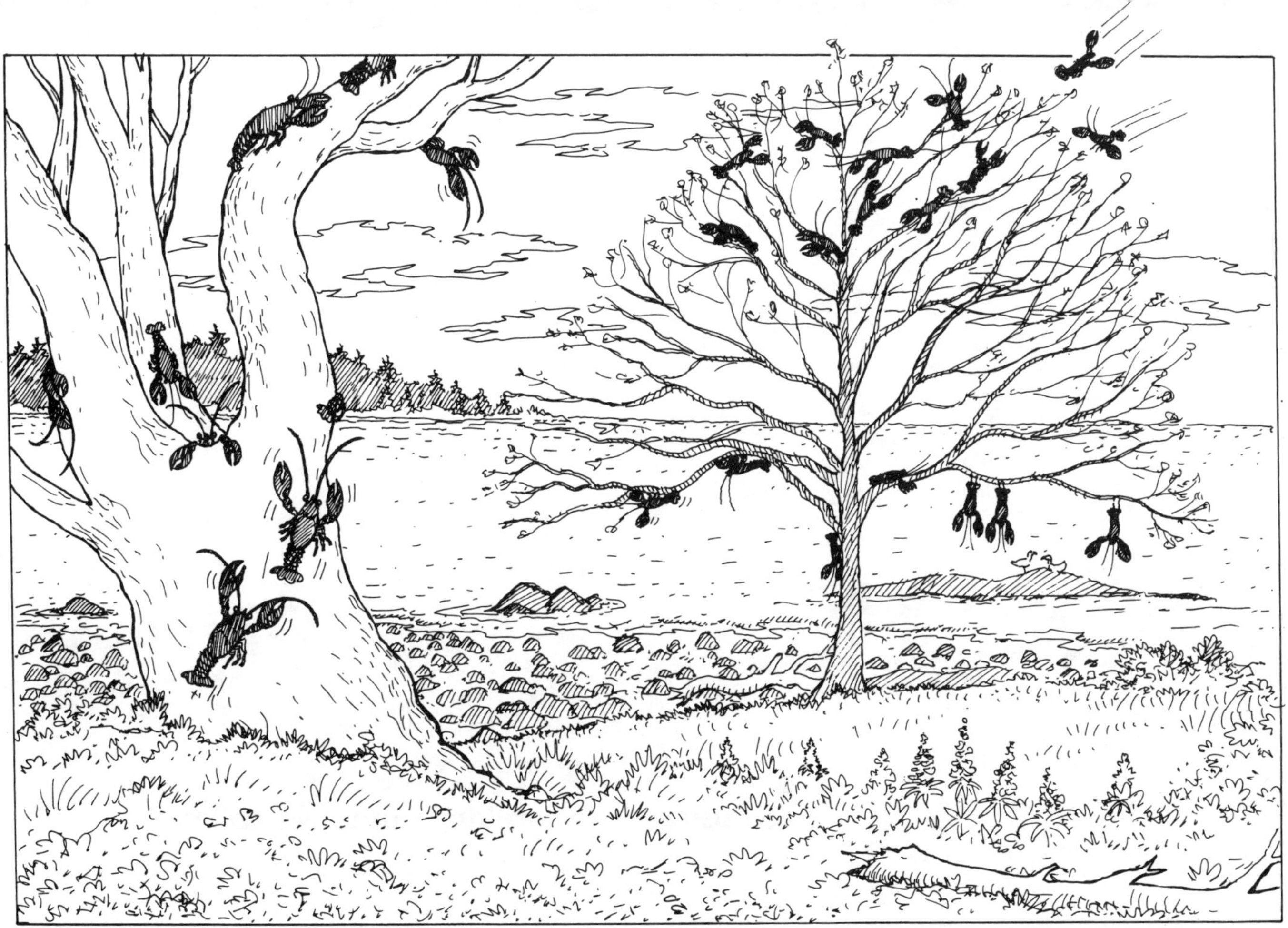

Lobsters enjoy seeking out new habitats.

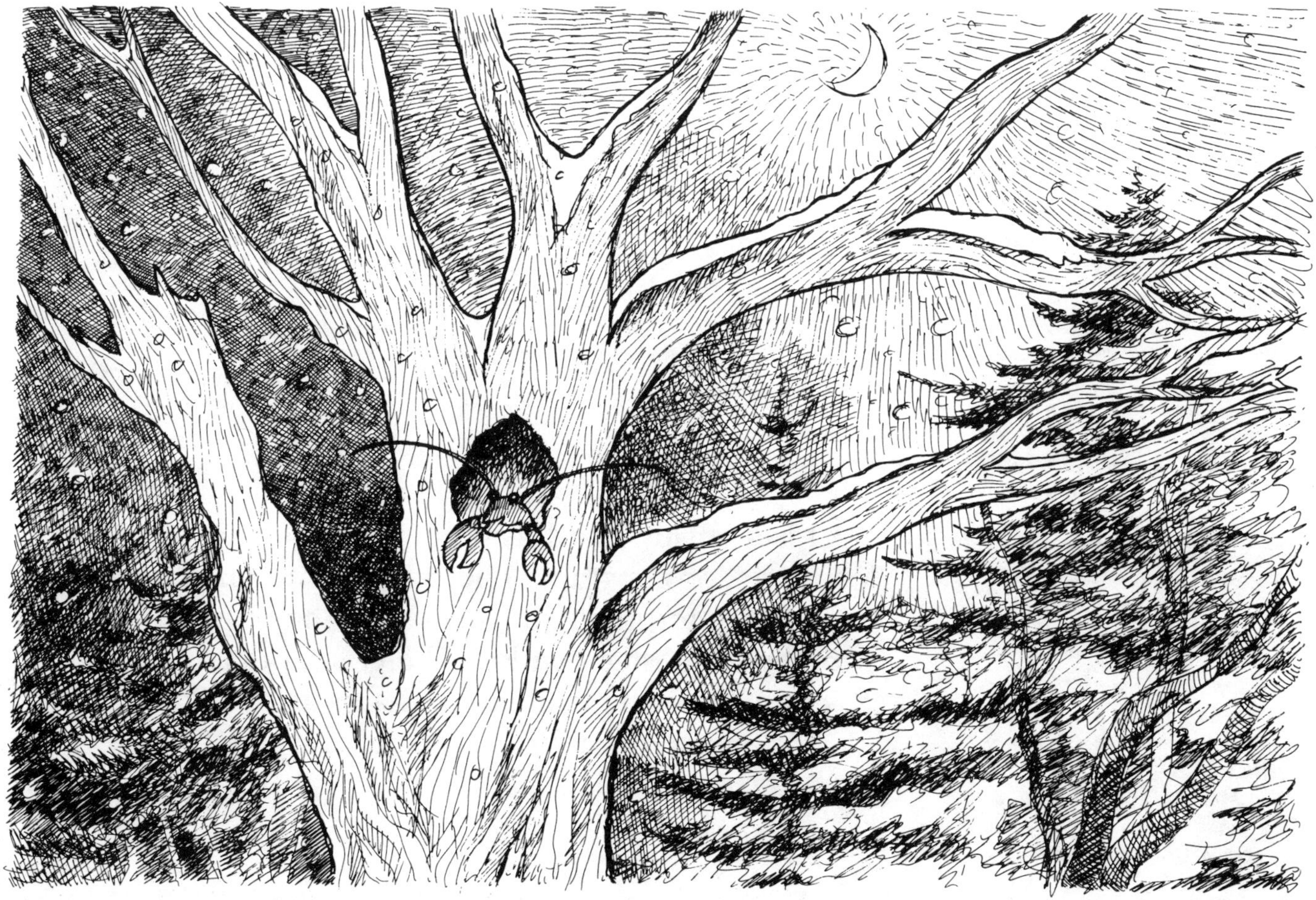

Lobster God?

Do Lobsters believe in God and what kind of religious experiences do they have? It turns out that their God is modeled after a lobsterman named Bob. Some lobsters say Bob is a kind and forgiving God, frequently setting them free after feeding them lavish meals, while others say Bob is a wrathful and vengeful God, throwing them into boiling water or baking them over hot coals.

Lobsters are often caught carrying little pictures of Bob and will use Bob's name in a number of ways. "Trust in Bob," "Let go and let Bob," "May Bob be with you," "With Bob, all things are possible," and for the little lobsters, "Remember, Bob is watching you."

Recent undersea photos taken in lobster territory have spotted a number of small lobster altars with statues of Bob.

Lobsters point out that one of the main reasons they feel their concept of God is superior to ours is because Bob spelled backwards is "Bob."

It is a fallacy that lobstermen occasionally lose their lobster traps. The truth of the matter is that enterprising lobsters steal the traps and build lobster condos. The going price is a 20-pound halibut, while time shares are available for choice food scraps, market varying.

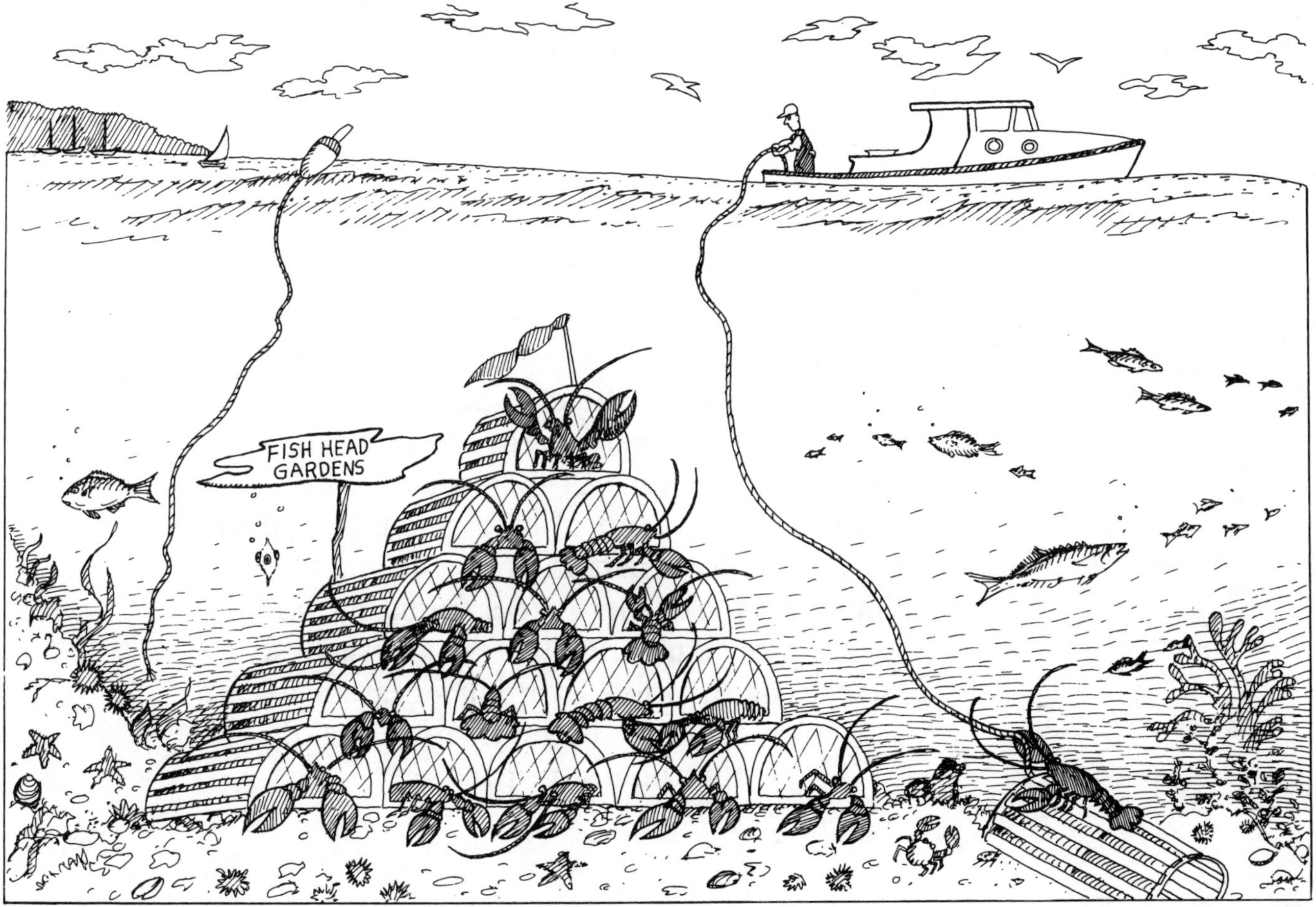
FISH HEAD
GARDENS

Where Maine License Plates Are Made

Did you know that Maine's license plate features a lobster logo? Will it surprise you to learn that they are made at a special lobster prison under the sea? This is where really bad lobsters go-- ones that are too mean to eat.

We've all heard of the "rogue elephant" or "rogue bear" that is antisocial and prone to unpredictable behavior. Visitors to coastal areas are cautioned to be on the lookout for "rogue" lobsters, whose favorite form of harassment is to drop down from overhanging branches onto their victims necks, causing quite a fright but no injury. Yuppies guard themselves against these unwelcome surprises by tying sweaters around their necks, enabling them to shake the rogues off promptly.

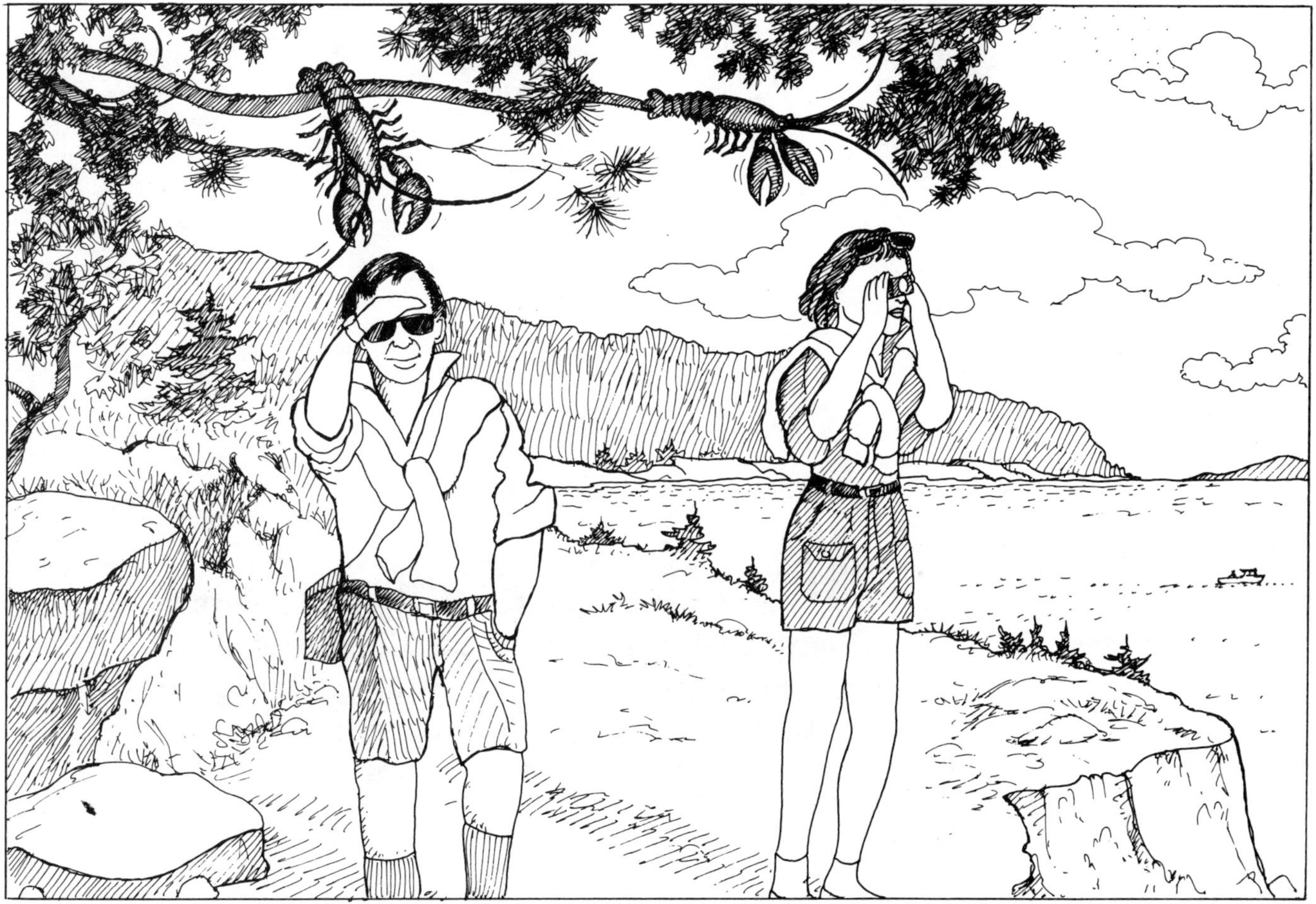

Everyone has to pitch in to make a farm a successful venture. "House" lobsters can be trained as "field" lobsters, earning their keep by participating in rototilling, pruning, and weed maintenance.

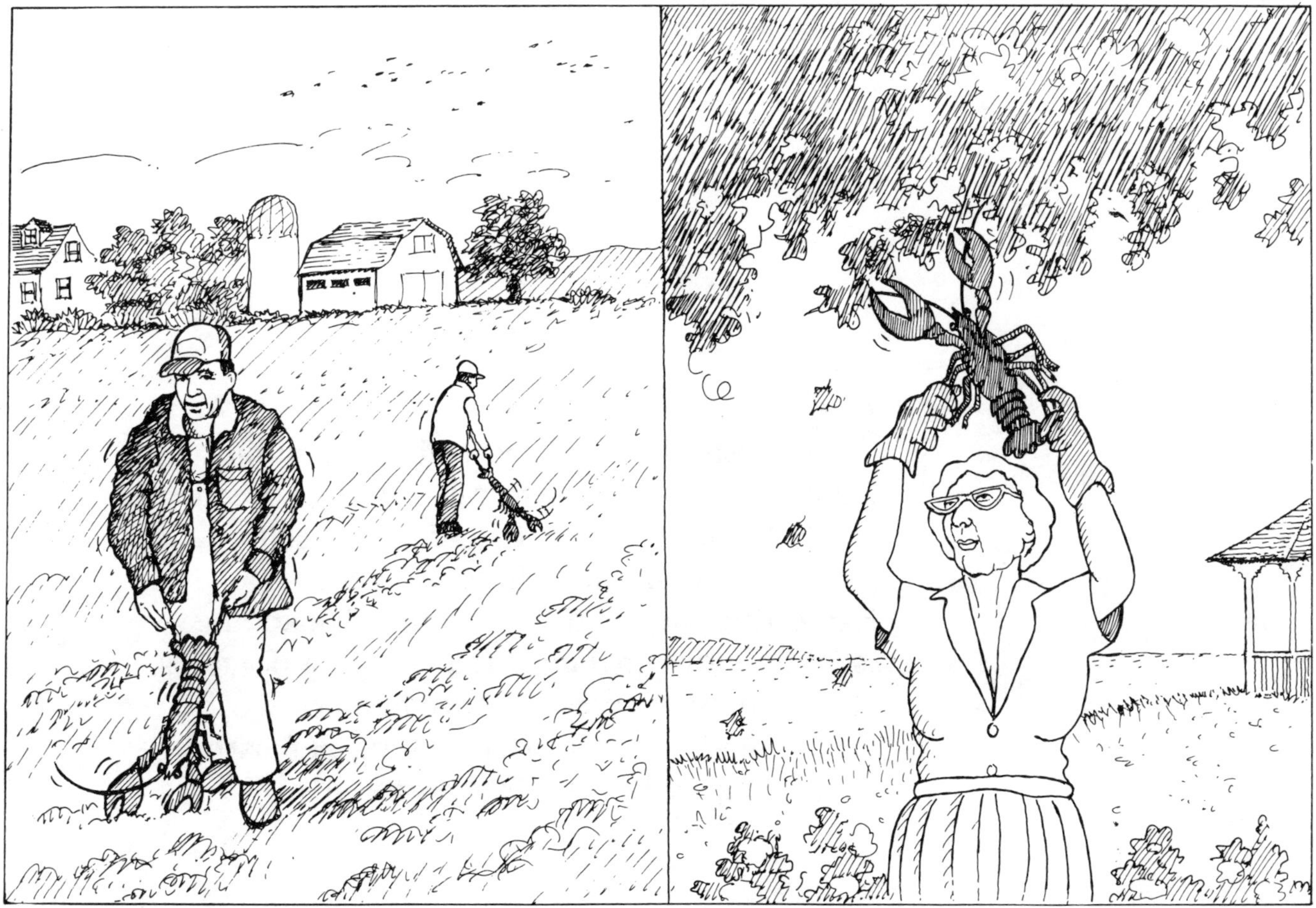

Aroostook County in Maine is famous
for its yearly potato harvest. A hearty breed
of "field" lobsters has adapted itself
to conditions here, as well.
Harvesting these exotic creatures is exciting,
presenting more challenge than digging potatoes.
During harvest season, entire families work
in the fields, the air often ringing out with
cries when a lobster is found.

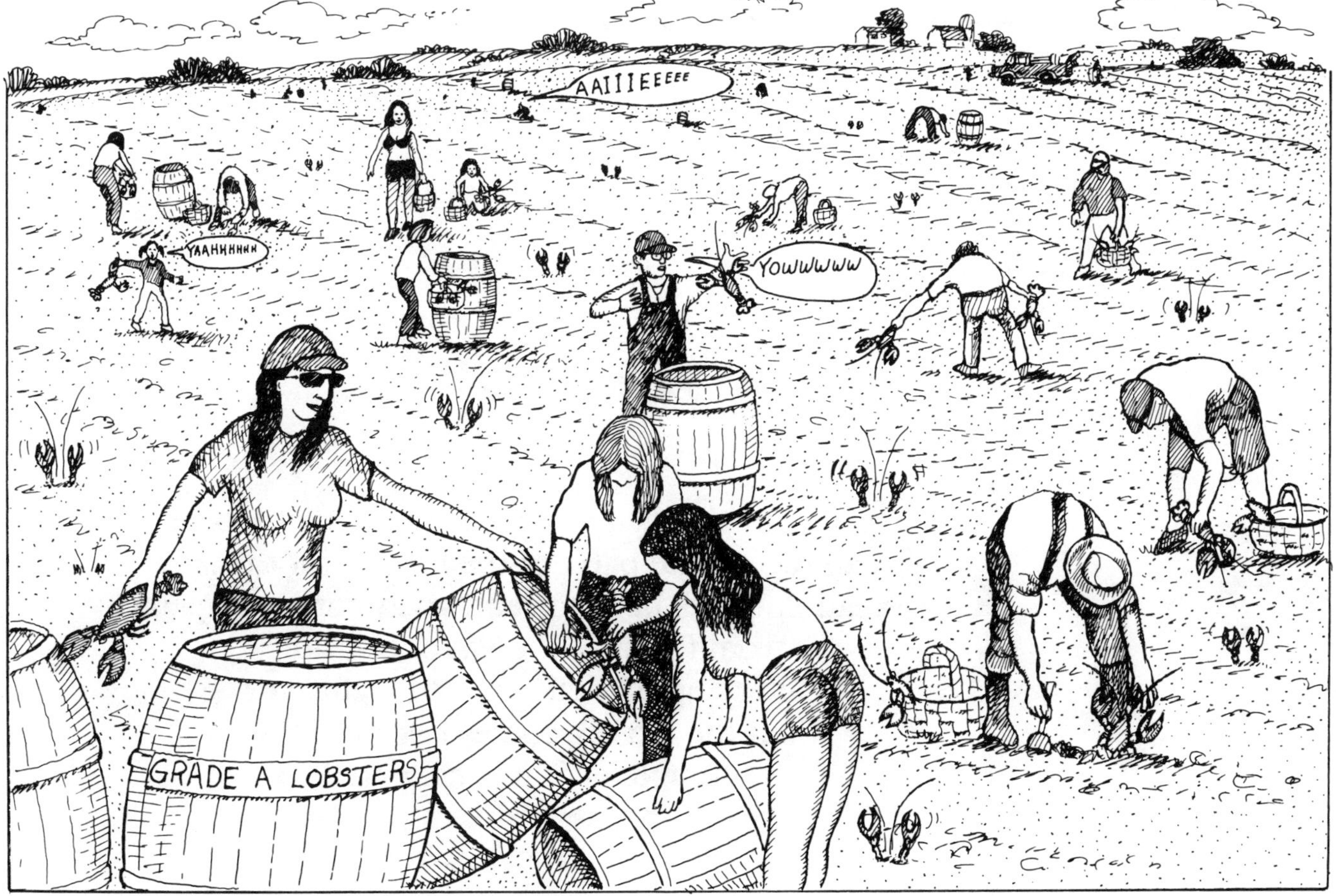
AAIIIEEEEE
YAAHHHHHH
YOWWWWW
GRADE A LOBSTERS

HARVESTING FIELD LOBSTERS

5

Strange but true

People are amazed when they hear that lobsters
can regenerate parts of their body. Not true.
Instead, lobsters have to send away for spare parts
from the *Whole Lobster Catalog*.
Delivery usually takes six to eight weeks;
then the lobster comes out of hiding
completely "regenerated."

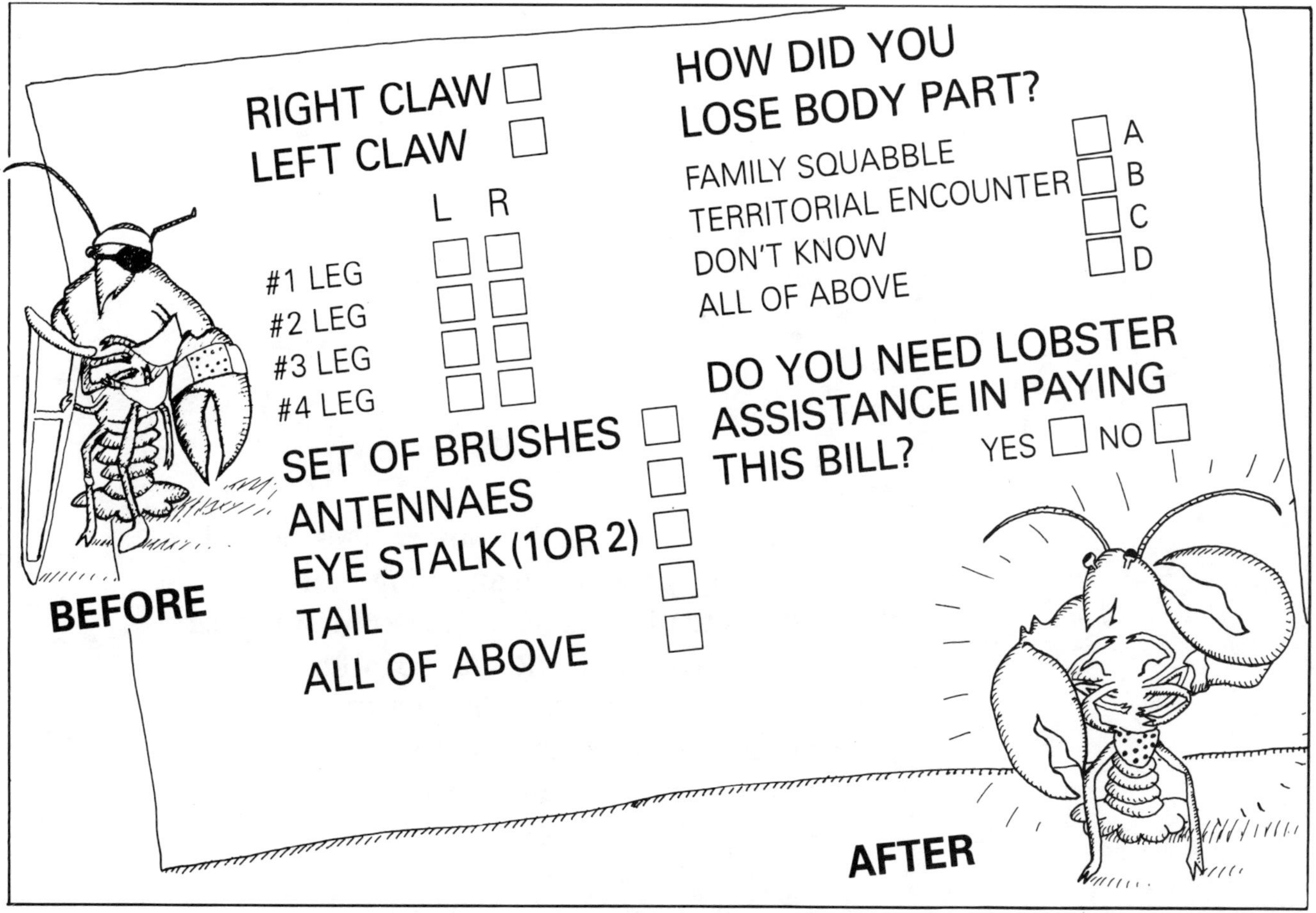

RIGHT CLAW ☐
LEFT CLAW ☐

	L	R
#1 LEG	☐	☐
#2 LEG	☐	☐
#3 LEG	☐	☐
#4 LEG	☐	☐

SET OF BRUSHES ☐
ANTENNAES ☐
EYE STALK (1 OR 2) ☐
TAIL ☐
ALL OF ABOVE ☐

BEFORE

HOW DID YOU
LOSE BODY PART?

FAMILY SQUABBLE ☐ A
TERRITORIAL ENCOUNTER ☐ B
DON'T KNOW ☐ C
ALL OF ABOVE ☐ D

DO YOU NEED LOBSTER
ASSISTANCE IN PAYING
THIS BILL?   YES ☐ NO ☐

AFTER

The Abominable Snow Lobster lives on a diet
of stray yaks and wandering natives.
While it is greatly feared, it is also highly prized.
It is said that one claw can feed
an entire wedding party.
Periodic trips over the mountains to China
are necessary to obtain giant rubber bands.

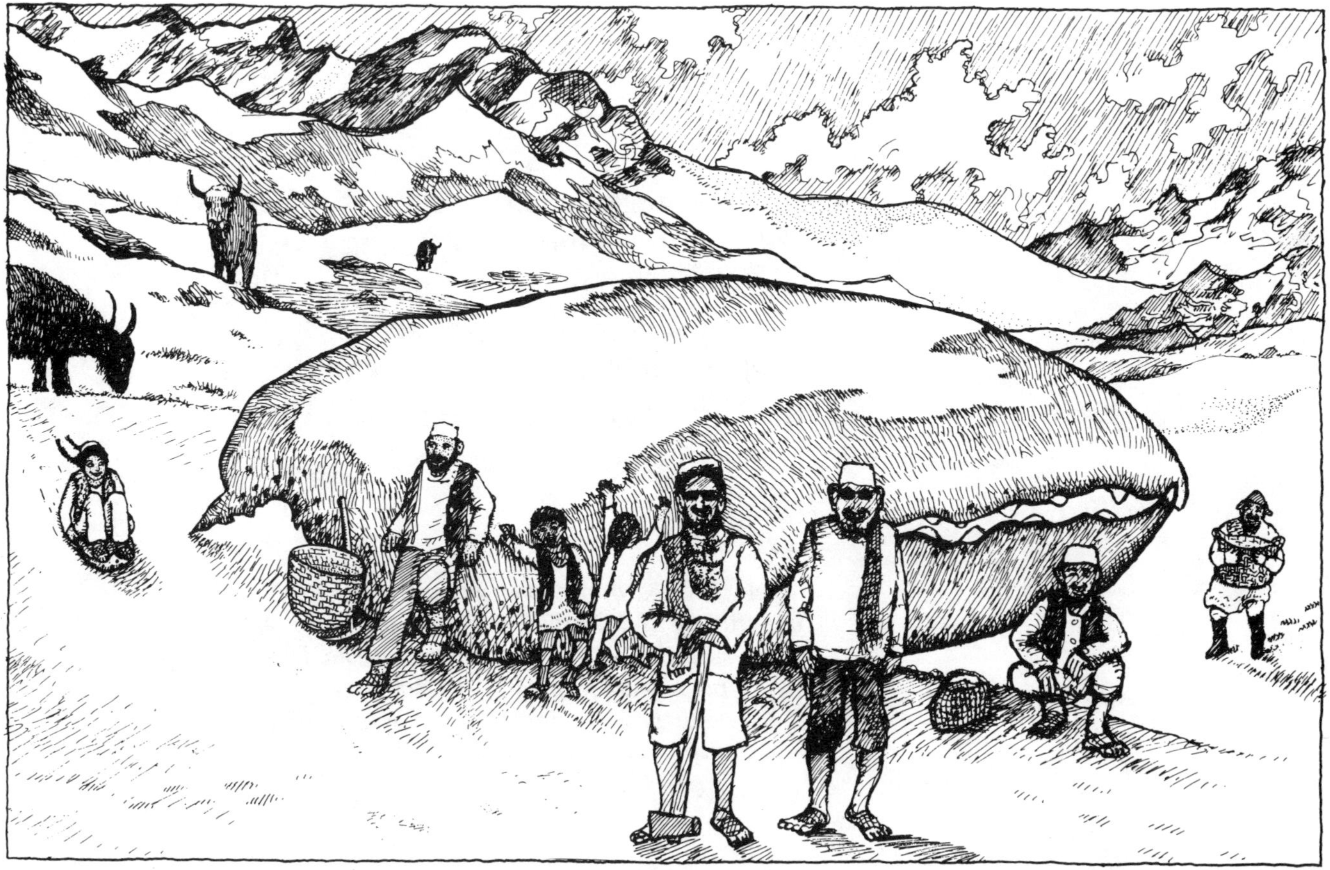

MAKING IT IN MAINE

Many lobstermen moonlight at other jobs
in the off season. One enterprising lobsterman
has started a mail-order business selling
packets of lobster seeds.
Planting instructions are simple
for the one, two and three-pound varieties.

*Put the seed in a flower pot and cover with
one inch of dirt. Mulch with seaweed and keep
moist with salt water. After two weeks, DO
NOT place your fingers in the dirt, but throw
in two large bugs daily. After three months
dump the whole pot into boiling water.*

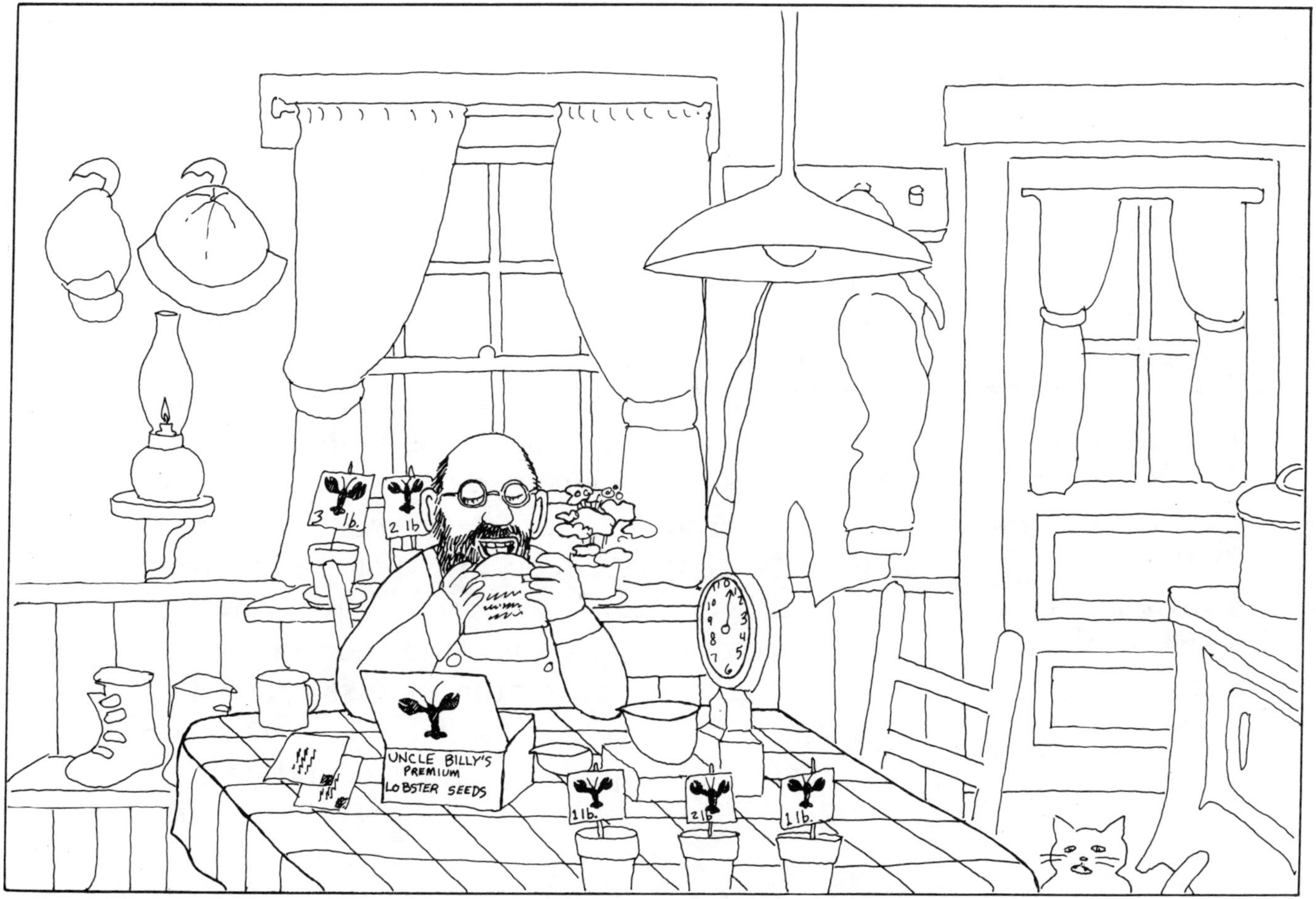
3 lb.
2 lb.
UNCLE BILLY'S PREMIUM LOBSTER SEEDS
1 lb.
2 lb.
1 lb.

Bonus Recipe

1- Boil a big pot of water.
2- Gather the family around the lobster and say goodbye to it.
3- Know deep in your heart that the lobster will get you back some day.
4- When you feel silly standing around staring at the lobster, drop it in the boiling water. Contrary to all the different opinions on how long it takes to cook a lobster, just take it out when you think it's done.
5- If you are really hungry you do not need instructions on how to eat it.

Why is it that lobsters can touch primal fears in some people? It is actually understandable. They look like giant spiders, have antennae and are always looking at you with those beady eyes—even when you're trying to eat them. For those who have never met a lobster, that first contact can be unsettling. People from the Midwest should study this picture carefully. If you come to Maine for a vacation and are going to eat lobster for the first time, try to practice other expressions than this. Your fellow diners will appreciate your thoughtfulness.

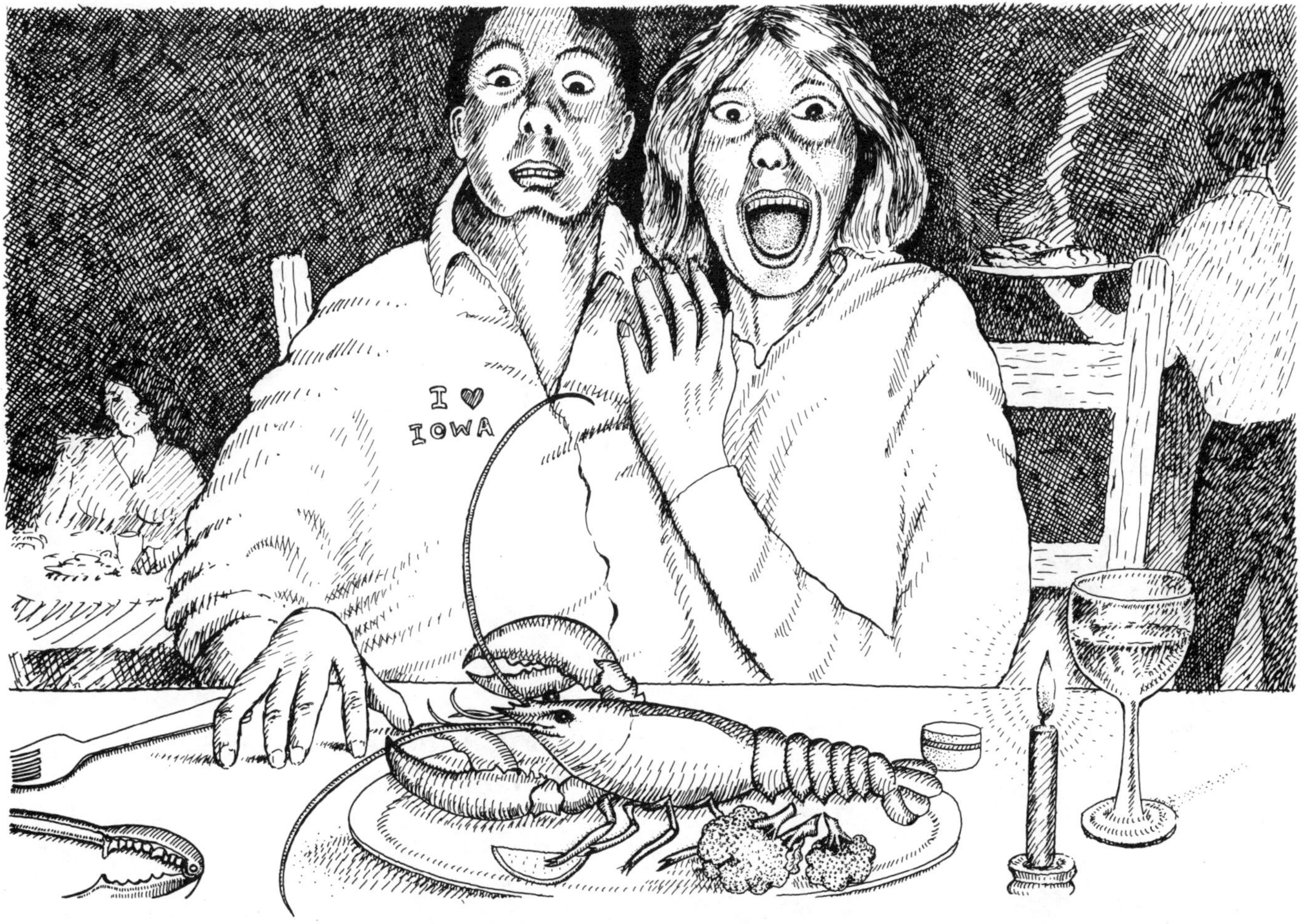
I ♥ IOWA

A Plea to Humanity

Maine has been battling giant ocean behemoths for years. There is such an abundance of these creatures that the state actually pays people to trap them. The only way to trim the population of this creature is to do the following:

Plunge it ALIVE into boiling water, then pull off its eight legs, crack open its formidable claws and then CONSUME ALL ITS FLESH.

When you visit Maine, this is how you can help. When you approach the toll booth at the Maine Turnpike, say to the toll operator, "I am here to battle the giant ocean behemoths."

You will be given a special kit to aid in this campaign. It will include a claw cracker, a little pick, a plastic fork, and a special bib with the behemoth emblazoned on it.

Just when you thought it was safe to come to Maine.

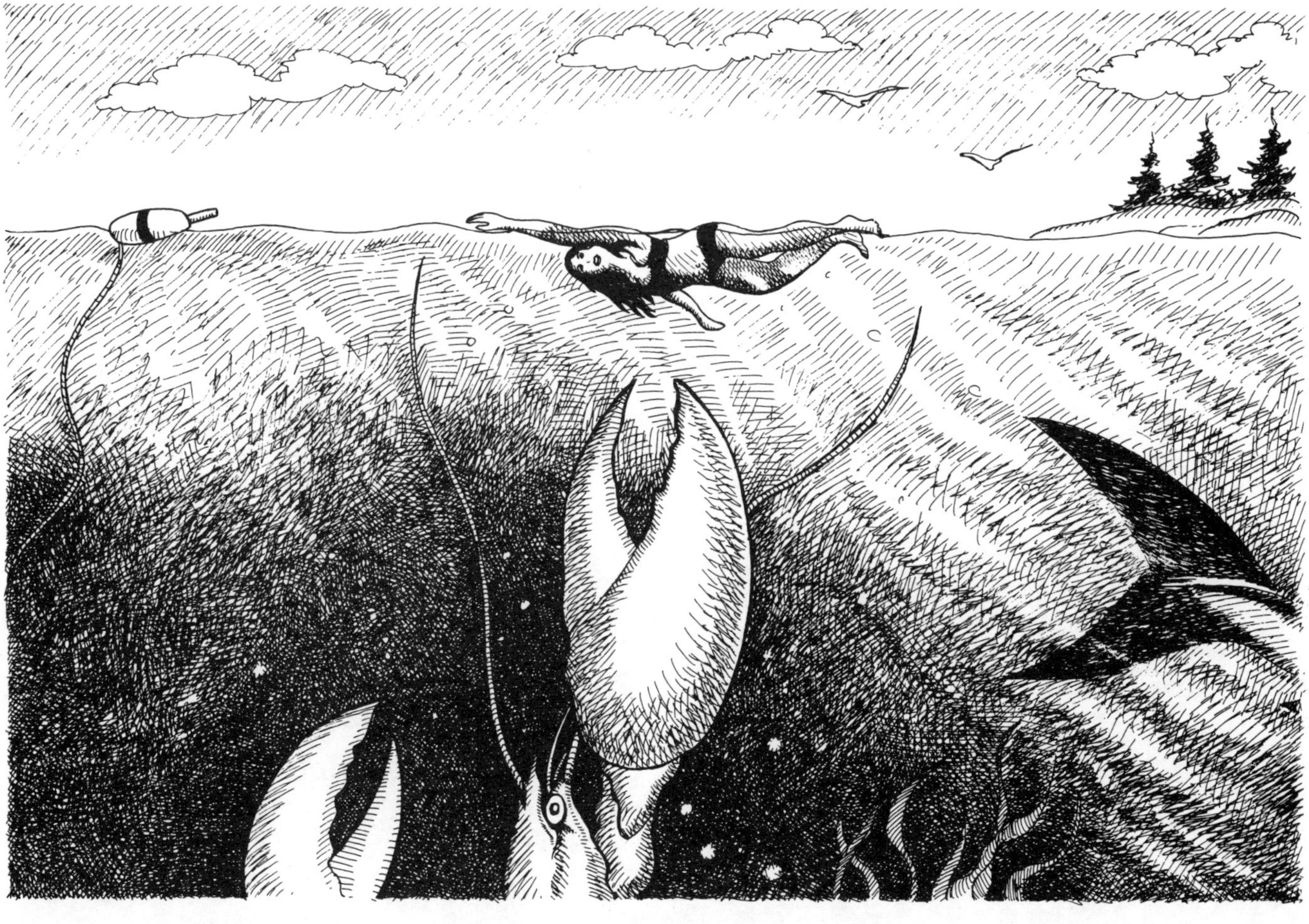

Common nightmares of people
after eating their first Maine lobster.

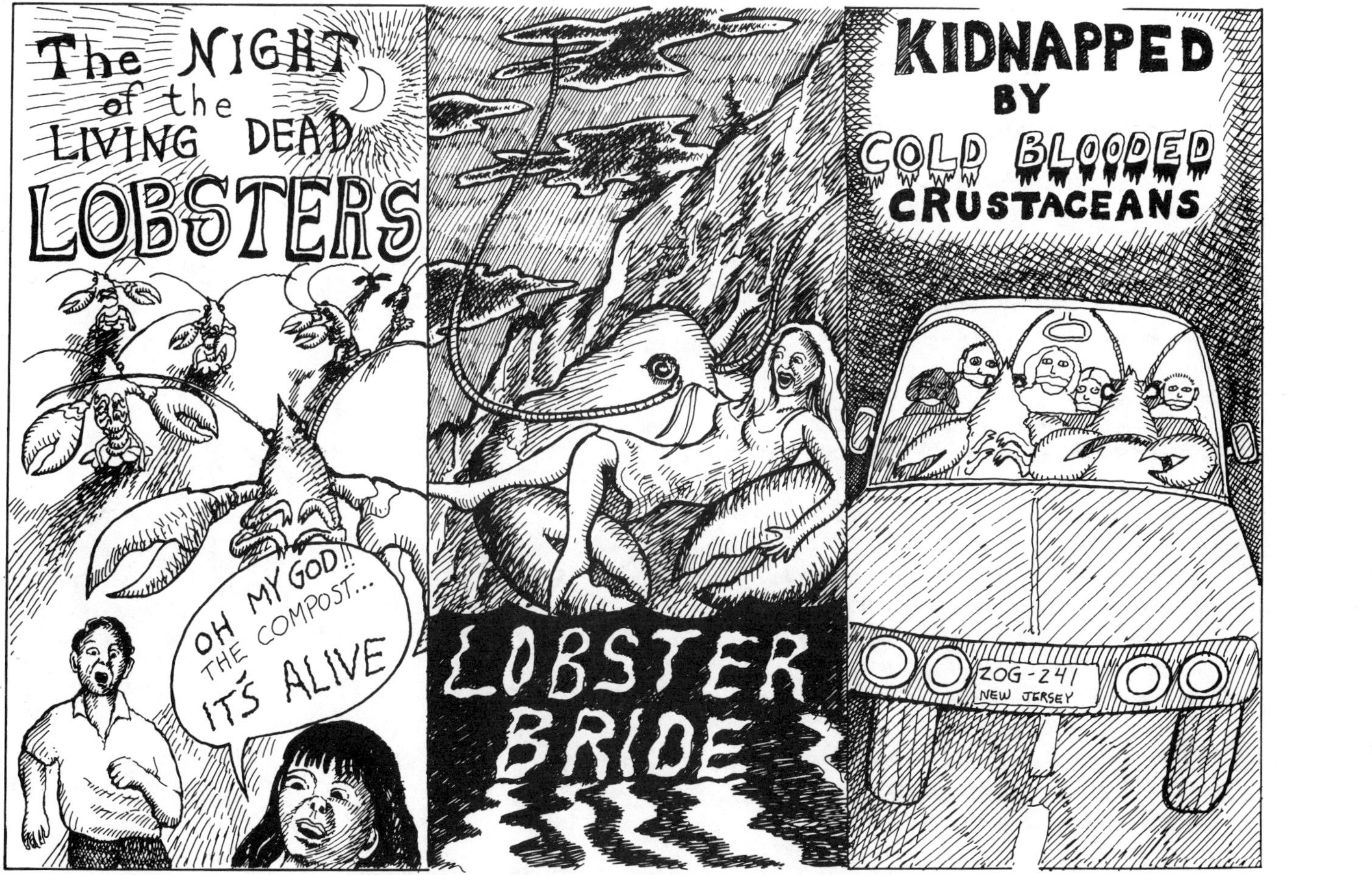
The NIGHT of the LIVING DEAD LOBSTERS
OH MY GOD!! THE COMPOST... IT'S ALIVE
LOBSTER BRIDE
KIDNAPPED BY COLD BLOODED CRUSTACEANS
ZOG-241
NEW JERSEY

How to Talk Lobster

By following these simple instructions, you can begin to communicate with lobsters on a basic level.

You will need: a special lobster cap with eyes and antennae as well as "claw" gloves. Both these items are available in most coastal gift shops.

As a precaution, wear sunglasses. It is now believed that lobsters possess awesome psychic powers. Lobstermen admit that lobsters have been hypnotizing them for years, making them perform silly tricks on their boats for hours on end.

You can practice your skills at lobster pounds, fish markets, restaurants and even airports— anywhere lobsters are on display. With enough practice, you'll be able to walk into any lobster pound with confidence and strike up a conversation with the lobsters.

Your skill could even lead to a valuable overseas job as an interpreter in such faraway places as Japan or France where lobsters are very popular.

"How much do you weigh?"

"Would you like to come over and try out my hot tub?"

"You are invited to a clambake. Just bring yourself and a friend."

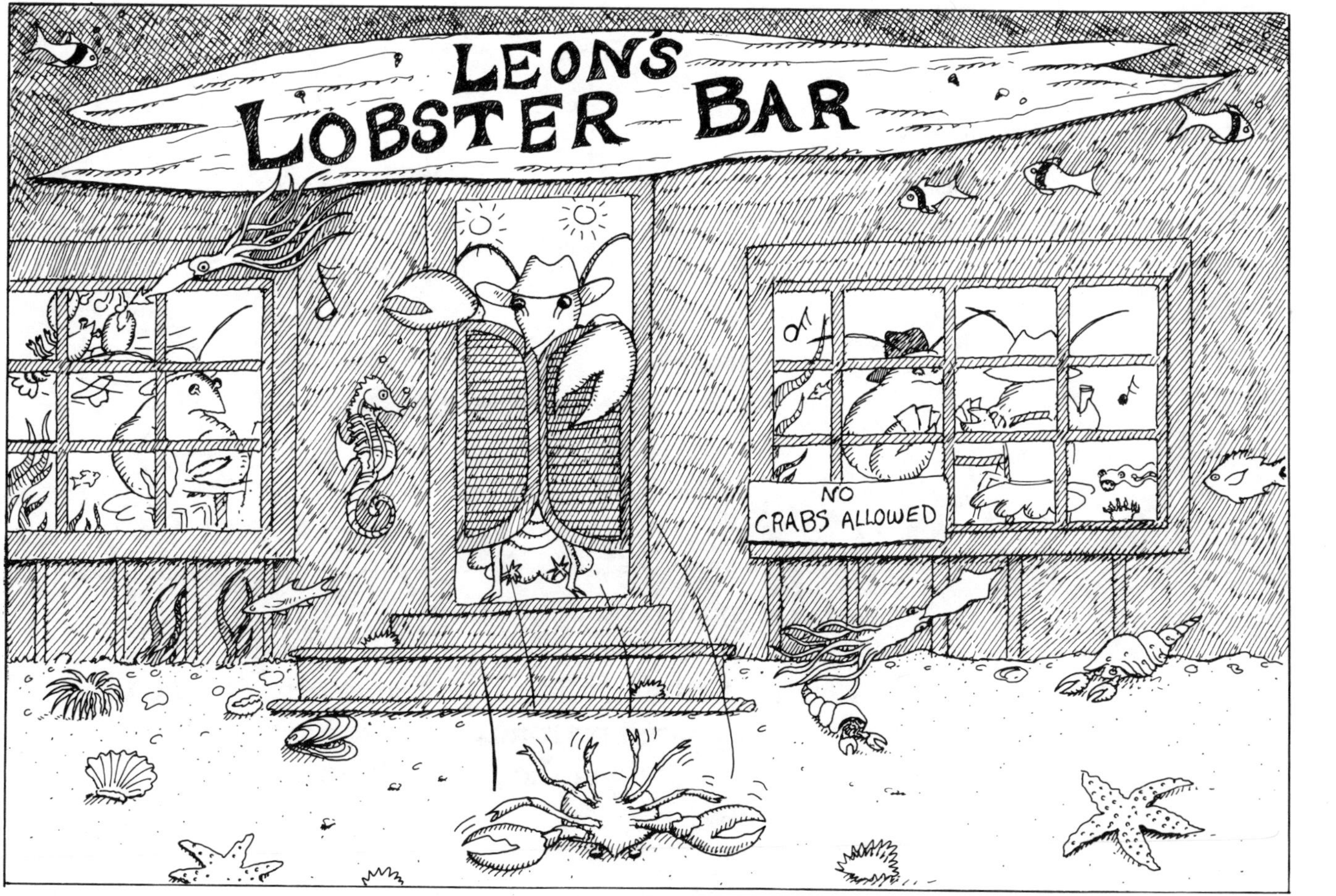
LEON'S
LOBSTER BAR
NO
CRABS ALLOWED

Lobsters are commonly referred to as scavengers, but given the choice they prefer a night out on the town with fine dining and entertainment.

Beneath their shells, lobsters have quite shapely and sexy bodies. Male lobsters get very excited when female lobsters begin to molt, and they often patronize little striptease joints along the ocean floor.

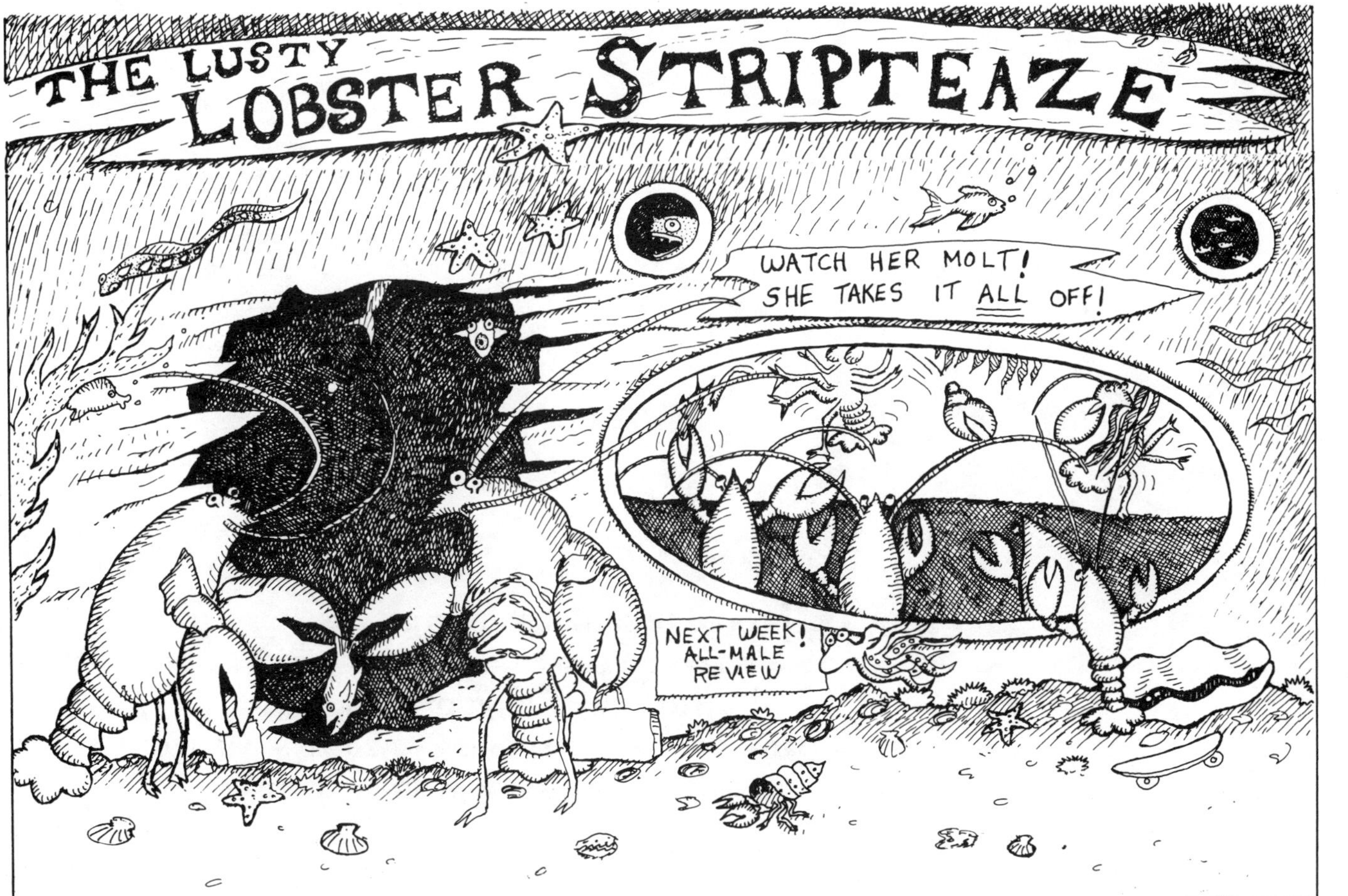
THE LUSTY LOBSTER STRIPTEAZE
WATCH HER MOLT! SHE TAKES IT ALL OFF!
NEXT WEEK! ALL-MALE REVIEW

George Bush doesn't forget his Texas past
when he comes to Maine. "Eat it?
Hell, no, I'm gonna ride it!
"Barb, get me my spurs. I've always wanted
to ride one of these Maine crawfish!"

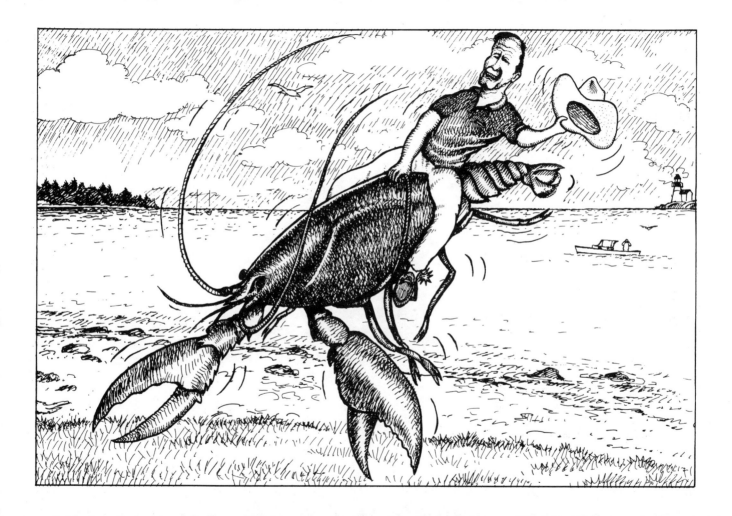

6

Getting closer
to your lobster

Lobsters' Mating Ritual

Lobsters' amazing mating rituals tie up traffic along the Maine coast every summer. Streaming up out of the ocean by the thousands, they cross the highway to mate and search for places to hide their eggs.

Within weeks, tiny lobsters emerge from their shells and make their perilous return to the sea. Only a small percentage will grow to maturity.

The following summer, on a moonlit night, the lobsters will return to the same stretch of beach and busy highway to fulfill their destiny.

Lobster love.

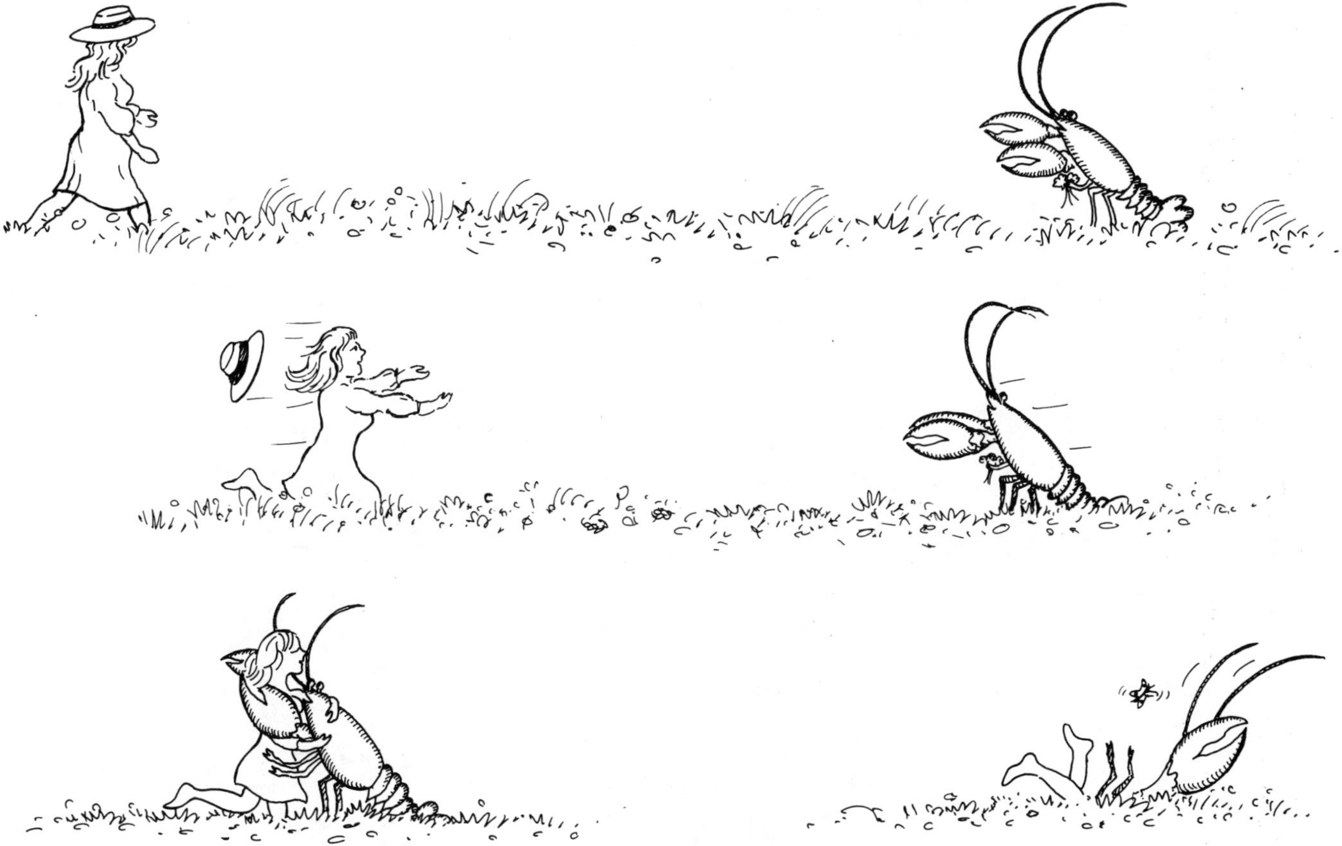

Hey, kids! Dress up your lobsters.
Simply cut out these clothes patterns, color,
use lots of sparkles, and surprise your parents.

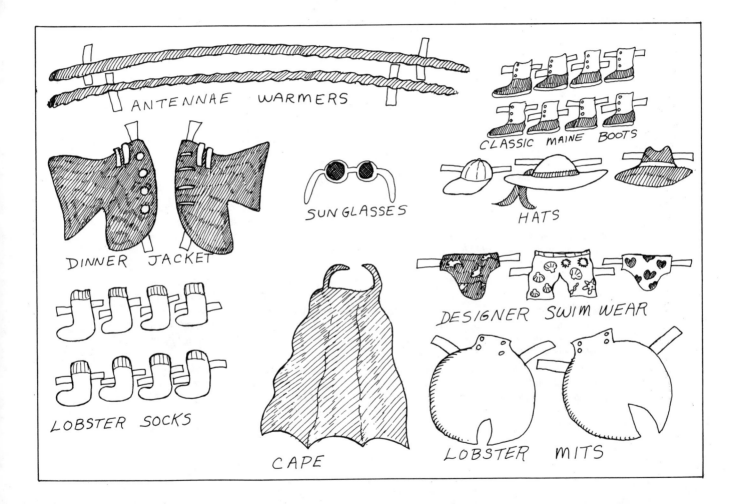

ANTENNAE WARMERS

CLASSIC MAINE BOOTS

DINNER JACKET

SUNGLASSES

HATS

LOBSTER SOCKS

DESIGNER SWIM WEAR

CAPE

LOBSTER MITS

Astrological Signs of Lobsters

This book would not be complete unless it dealt with the important field of lobster astrology.

When you walk into a lobster pound there are two important questions you ask: "How much does that lobster weigh?" and "How much does that lobster cost?" But how often have you wanted to ask, "What is that lobster's astrological sign?" How do you determine a lobster's sign when you stare into a tank of entangled claws and tails?

In the wild, it is far easier. Sagittarian lobsters carry little bows and arrows; Libra lobsters carry a little set of scales and are forever weighing their food scraps, "too much, too little," until the scales are balanced and they can eat. Leo lobsters are quite proud and brazen and have no qualms about striding up on the beach and bumming cigarettes, spare change and food scraps.

Spotting signs in the lobster tank can be more confusing, but here are some tips: That pile of lobsters in the corner? All legs and claws intertwined? You can be certain they're Aquarians because they love a crowd.

Actually, the simplest way to determine signs is to ask. Lobstermen have changed with the times. They are familiar with fine wines and well-versed in lobster signs.

Just stride up to the counter, smile and say in a bold voice, "Yes, I'd like a two-pound Aquarian lobster."

"Do you have any Capricorns today?" You will be surprised how the lobsterman brightens up and begins a spirited discussion of the merits of various signs.

David Hurley lives in Swanville, Maine with his wife Sheila and three sons, Chris, Matt, and Willie. He was born in Fontainbleau, France. One of his first words was "Homard" (French word for Lobster). Raised in the suburbs of New Jersey, he escaped in 1980 to settle in Maine. He has a studio in Belfast where he takes naps and creates great art. In his spare time he is a bartender, waiter, housepainter, and delivers newspapers one day a week.